IN GOOD
COMPANY

D1016179

Fratribus carissimis in Societate Jesu

IN GOOD COMPANY

THE FAST TRACK FROM THE CORPORATE WORLD
TO POVERTY, CHASTITY AND OBEDIENCE

10th Anniversary Edition

JAMES MARTIN, S.J.

SHEED & WARD

Lanham, Boulder, New York, Toronto, and Plymouth, UK

Published by Sheed & Ward
An imprint of Rowman & Littlefield Publishers, Inc.
A wholly owned subsidary of The Rowman & Littlefield Publishing Group, Inc.
4501 Forbes Boulevard, Suite 200
Lanham, MD 20706

Estover Road, Plymouth PL6 7PY, United Kingdom

Distributed by National Book Network

Copyright © 2000 by The Society of Jesus of New England
Introduction to the tenth anniversary edition © 2010 by
The Society of Jesus of New England

Imprimi potest:
Very Rev. Robert Levens, S.J.
Provincial, The Society of Jesus
New England Province

Interior design: GrafixStudio, Inc.

Scripture quotations are from the Revised Standard Version of the Bible, copyright
1946, 1952, and 1972 by the Division of Christian Education of the National Council
of the Churches of Christ in the USA. Used by permission. All rights reserved.

All rights reserved. No part of this publication may be reproduced, stored in a retrieval
system, or transmitted in any form or by any means, electronic, mechanical, photocopying,
recording, or otherwise, without the prior permission of the publisher, except by a reviewer
who may quote passages in a review.

Library of Congress Cataloging-in-Publication Data

The previous edition of this book was cataloged by the Library of Congress as follows:

Martin, James, S.J.
  In good company : the fast track from the corporate world to
    poverty, chastity and obedience / James Martin.
      p.   cm.
    Martin, James, S.J.   2. Jesuits—United States—Biography.
3. Missionaries—Kenya—Nairobi—Biography.   4. Missionaries—
United States—Biography.   I. Title.

BX4705 .M41243   A3   2000
271'.5302—dc21

                                                    00-041968

    ISBN 978-1-58051-236-7 (pbk. : alk. paper)
    ISBN 978-1-58051-237-4 (electronic)

Printed in the United States of America.

⊗™ The paper used in this publication meets the minimum requirements of
American National Standard for Information Sciences—Permanence of
Paper for Printed Library Materials, ANSI/NISO Z39.48-1992.

Contents

❧

Introduction to the 10th Anniversary Edition ix

Part I
Restless Hearts

1. Leges Sine Moribus Vanae 3
2. Petals on a Bough 27
3. An Unseen Hook 47

Part II
Come and See

4. A Bruised Reed 71
5. The Sign of Jonas 97
6. The Manner Is Ordinary 109

Part III
Late Have I Loved You

7. Religious by Nature 131
8. Simple Tasks 151
9. Seeing Life Whole 173

Acknowledgments 203

Introduction to the 10th Anniversary Edition

This is the book of a young man, or at least a younger one. A few years after entering the Jesuits in 1988, I was sent to work in East Africa. My job was to help refugees who had settled in Nairobi, Kenya, start small business to support themselves. But after too much work and too little sleep, I ended up with a bout of mononucleosis. "You traveled halfway around the world to get *that*?" joked a friend. "You could have gotten that in college!"

The local doctor was strict: two months of bed rest and no work. But after two weeks, and reading through most of the books we had in our Jesuit house library, I found that I had an enormous amount of time on my hands. So I started to write this account of my leaving the corporate world and entering the Jesuits. I wanted to get the story down before I forgot the details: the sights, the sounds, the emotions—and, especially, the conversations. After I recovered, I stored the book on a computer disk and forgot about the manuscript.

Eight years later, after I published a book on my time in East Africa, a friend at Sheed & Ward asked if had any other writing projects I might be interested in publishing. So I fished out the old computer disk and sent it along, but not before printing out a copy of the manuscript. Reading it again was something of a shock, somewhat akin to hearing yourself on an old tape recording, or seeing yourself on an old video. It's you of course, but it's also a markedly different person.

Rather than revising the manuscript, I decided to leave it essentially untouched, preferring instead to let that younger person—still fresh with memories of the first stirrings of a vocation, still carrying the glow of the novitiate, still full of definite (and rather strong) opinions about life in a religious order, that is, still very much a *new* Jesuit—tell the story the way he saw it all those years ago.

When I read the book today, ten years after the first edition came out, I can see how much has changed. For one thing, I see the story through a different lens now.

At the time, if someone had asked what led me to enter the Jesuits, I would have answered like this: I was miserable in my job and discovered a lifeline, a wonderful new way to live. And that's true. God offered me a way out. Now, however, I would describe things using a more overtly spiritual vocabulary. What happened to me is what happens in all "vocation" stories: God called me through desire.

The word "vocation" comes from the Latin word *vocare*, meaning "to call." So a vocation is something you are called to. And everyone has a vocation. It may be as a doctor, lawyer or business person; or as a mother or father; or as a priest or member of a religious order. We are drawn to these vocations primarily through our deep desires, which we discover over time or sometimes all at once: we find that we are attracted to a particular way of life. On the most basic level, a husband and wife are drawn together out of desire—physical, emotional, spiritual—and discover their vocations as a married couple. A young man or woman might study with an inspiring teacher and feel an attraction to teaching. God works through our desires.

In the midst of those difficult, stressful days at work, I found myself—thanks to a television show, of all things—drawn to consider life in a religious order. A documentary on the Trappist monk Thomas Merton led me to think about doing something else with my life, though I had little idea what that "something else" would be. All of this, in other words, came from an inchoate longing for something beautiful. God often works in our lives through these heartfelt desires, including those that may be difficult to explain to others, or even understand ourselves.

But from that unformed longing God was able to work. In time, God gave me an answer to a question I hadn't even asked.

* * *

OVER THE LAST TEN YEARS, this book has been used by, among other people, seekers, believers, doubters, agnostics and atheists—not to mention reading groups, high school and college classes, as well as people interested in the priesthood and life in a religious order. (And their parents, too: many Jesuits have told me that they have given this book to their parents as a way of saying, "Look, entering a religious order is not so crazy!") Since then, I've also gotten cards and letters from readers asking what happened in the intervening years.

So a few updates may be in order.

First, I've completed my Jesuit training—finally! This book ends on the day of my first vows, which come after a Jesuit has completed his two years of novitiate training. After that came two years studying philosophy at Loyola University Chicago; two years of work in East Africa; one year at *America*, a Catholic magazine in New York City; and three years of theology studies in Cambridge, Mass. After ordination to the priesthood in 1999, I returned to *America*, as an associate editor. And, just a few months ago, I formally finished my Jesuit training and pronounced my "final vows."

Second, my family has grown much more comfortable with my vocation as a Jesuit. My mother and sister (and now brother-in-law and two nephews) are all wonderfully supportive. (My father died in 2001, but before his death he was just as enthusiastic as the rest of my family.) Overall, the confused reactions of my family described in this book wore off almost as soon as they got to know individual Jesuits. Now they are great fans of the Jesuits. My friends, too, are entirely supportive and, along with my family, rejoiced with me at my ordination and final vow Masses.

Third, I've changed the way I look at the corporate world. One of the concerns I heard when this book came out was that it contained too severe a critique of the corporate world. Some readers wrote to say that for them business is every bit as much of a vocation as is one to a religious order—which is true. So an explanation: everything I wrote about my time in corporate America is accurate, in the sense that it happened the way I describe. But it is not normative. Not every business environment is exactly like what I encountered during my six years at General Electric. Nonetheless, as I said, it is an accurate account of one man's experience.

Overall, I'm delighted that this book is still helping people understand something about prayer, about service to the poor, about religious orders, about the priesthood, about the Jesuits, and even about Christianity and Catholicism in general. But I hope that it helps you in a broader way: to discover your own path in life, to find God in all things, and to learn that you, too, are called to something special in life, to a unique vocation that God has fashioned for you before you were born.

And now, let me turn things over to that much younger man, who will tell you his story as he saw it all those years ago in East Africa during his long, idle weeks of convalescence.

James Martin, S.J.

July 31, 2010
Feast of St. Ignatius Loyola

Part I

Restless Hearts

*You have made us for yourself, Lord, and our hearts
are restless until they rest in you.*

St. Augustine, *Confessions*

1.
Leges Sine Moribus Vanae

Laws without morals are useless.

Motto of the University of Pennsylvania

There is a hospice in Kingston, Jamaica, called Our Lady Queen of Peace. The two-story concrete building, painted a cheerful blue and white, is home to the Missionaries of Charity, a women's religious order perhaps best known for its foundress, Mother Teresa of Calcutta. To reach the hospice you must walk through one of the larger slums of Kingston, where mangy goats, surly roosters, scrawny chickens, and the occasional pig root through small mountains of garbage left rotting on the streets. In the mornings, crowds of uniformed Jamaican children, their bleached white shirts highlighting brown faces, run through hot streets on their way to school. While street gangs hold sway over the neighbors, they leave untroubled the sisters at the hospice.

The sisters care for the sick and dying in Kingston. Every morning they set out, wearing their distinctive habits—blue-and-white saris—to locate people who are too sick to care for themselves. Many times they carry the sick back to the hospice, where they are bathed, clothed, and given food and a place to stay, often to die. The men sleep in one wing, women in another. It is a bright, pleasant place, with an ample courtyard open to the Jamaican sun. After the midday rains, the residents sit in the atrium as the sisters wash the soiled linens and the green lizards sun themselves lazily.

One morning, when I was working in this hospice, a friend arrived from the United States. At the time, I was busy showering and dressing a dozen old men who were too ill to wash themselves. My job was to clean as many men as I could before their noon meal. Sometimes I also shaved them and clipped their fingernails and toenails, a job I particularly disliked.

I worked in a large communal bathroom, with cracked porcelain toilets along one wall and showers along another. The men who were unable to stand I washed using a bucket of water and a sponge, while they sat on a makeshift metal chair with a plastic toilet seat fastened to its top. I knelt on a floor covered with water from the showers and urine from the overflowing toilets. The sisters used a large concrete sink in the bathroom for their laundry, where they washed their saris along with the hospice's bed linens in a strong, pungent bleach. The bathroom, therefore, smelled like excrement, urine, bleach, and soap. I was holding my breath.

I was also trying, rather unsuccessfully, to help one of the old men pull on his pants—already wet from lying on the floor—over the sodden shoes that he had insisted on wearing in the shower.

It was damp and hot in the bathroom, and I was sweating. A reflection shimmered on the wet tile floor. I looked up and saw my friend watching me through the bathroom door, silhouetted by the bright light that streamed in from the courtyard. He stared for a few seconds and said, "Boy, if your friends from Wharton could see you now."

IT'S STILL DIFFICULT for me to believe that I found myself working in a Kingston ghetto after a six-year career in corporate finance. Perhaps even more surprising, I was working at the hospice as a novice of the Society of Jesus, the Roman Catholic religious order also known as the Jesuits. As part of a ten-year preparation period for ordination to the priesthood, I spent a good deal of time working among the poor. And, at a point in life when I expected to have a high-paying job, a career, a house, a family, and a car (or two), I had, instead, none of those things.

I did not come from a very religious family, at least not the kind that considers themselves "blessed" if a son decides to become a priest. My parents were both Catholics—my father had even attended Catholic schools—and they were married in the Catholic Church. My sister Carolyn and I were baptized and confirmed. When I was a young boy, we ate fish on Fridays and throughout Lent, and would never dream of missing Mass on Christmas or Easter. But my parents' love of God did not manifest itself in the religious practices favored by devout Catholics, that is, grace at mealtimes, daily Mass, family prayers, recitations of the rosary, and the like. Rather, they showed their desire to be good Christian parents in other ways: nursing their children to health when they were sick; teaching them how to throw a football or ride a bike; helping them with their homework; driving them to Cub Scout and Brownie meetings; and cheering them on at school plays. In other words, by loving and encouraging my sister and me.

But if my parents were only occasional churchgoers, they were nevertheless insistent that *I* attend Mass and Sunday School, or in Catholic parlance, Confraternity of Christian Doctrine—C.C.D. Religion was therefore an obligation of childhood. Like doing your homework, making your bed and taking out the trash.

Like most Catholic children, I endured C.C.D. lessons for the few years before first holy Communion and confirmation. Attending C.C.D. involved going to Sunday-morning classes taught by the nuns at our local parish school. I had, of course, passed the Catholic students on the way to my own public school in the morning—the girls in green-and-blue pleated kilts and the boys in navy blazers with gold buttons and white crests. But neither I nor any of my friends knew any parochial school kids. They seemed a separate, higher, caste—and this made the experience of sitting at their desks on Sundays after Mass vaguely frightening.

Epiphany of Our Lord School was not at all like my own public school. The youngish, mini-skirted teachers at Ridge Park Elementary School were nothing like the imperious nuns at Epiphany, who wore full black habits with long rosary beads hanging from their waists. Strange, polychromed plaster statues stood in strange-smelling tiled hallways. The lárgest was a four-foot high statue of Mary, who gazed out at her charges while, from under her pale blue dress, a rosy foot peeped out to crush a snake gagging on an apple. Why were the desks bolted together? I wondered. And why did they have circular holes in the top of them? I could fit my hand through the hole to root through the desks (which I did frequently). And when nuns weren't watching (which was infrequently) I would open the hinged desktop to examine neat piles of books and pens inside. A few years later someone told me that the nuns at his Catholic school instructed the students to tidy their desks every Friday afternoon, lest the "publics" look through them on Sundays and think them sloppy.

I remained in C.C.D. just long enough to qualify for first holy Communion and confirmation. The latter ceremony was celebrated by John Cardinal Krol, then the archbishop of Philadelphia. He visited our church very much as I thought God would have, wearing a tall miter, bearing a polished golden crozier, and pulling a five-foot scarlet train held aloft by five or six priests. I liked confirmation since I could pick a new confirmation name, Thomas, which went between my middle name and last name. I was nine years old.

As at first holy Communion the year before, the boys wore new brown or black suits complemented by a sporty white tie fastened with an elastic band that stretched around the collar. The girls wore white dresses and matching veils. My parents took me to Sears to have a picture taken of me in my brown suit; I knelt on a white table and held black rosary beads between my folded hands. In the weeks preceding the Big Day, I received religious cards and gifts—Bibles, rosary beads, and an occasional ten-dollar bill that would fall out of the odd card like a leaf dropping from a branch. Although I didn't get to pick a new name at Communion, I finally was able to eat the Eucharist, which tasted like cardboard. It was disrespectful to chew the Body of Christ, the nuns told us. You were to receive it on your tongue and immediately press it against the roof of your mouth and let it melt.

Shortly after confirmation, however, I began to lose interest in C.C.D. The weekly lessons seemed to grow duller by the month: one year was entirely given over to learning about the Old Testament, and I could never remember which prophet was which. So I decided I wanted out. The classes were boring, I was scared of the nuns, I didn't know many of the other kids in class, and I hated spending an extra hour on Sunday mornings in, of all places, school. Besides, why did I need to know anything about Isaiah? I figured I had already gotten what I needed—Communion and confirmation—and so I begged my parents not to send me any longer. After I begged long (and loud) enough, they agreed.

My religious education, then, lasted only a few years, and my understanding of religion was therefore frozen at what I had learned by age ten. So, like many of my friends, I grew up equipped with only a child's view of religion and faith. And while it's salutary to know, say, the definition of a mortal sin and a sacrament at age ten, one needs considerably more education to make it through life as an adult.

To assist the families in our parish with their moral and religious development, a priest visited each house in the neighborhood once a year. This was called the "visitation." One night, usually during the school year, one of the priests from Epiphany would drop by after dinner. We served him milk and cake from the A&P. One year, our visitor was the recently ordained Father Sheehan, who was called, at least in our house, the "hippie priest," because he rode a motorcycle, wore a leather jacket, and had sideburns. It was said that the scar he carried on his right cheek was the result of a bar fight.

Father Sheehan asked my parents questions designed to ascertain what kind of Catholic family we were. Did we go to

Mass? Did my sister and I still go to C.C.D.? How often did we go to confession? Did we receive the Eucharist regularly? How much did we donate to the church? My parents chatted amiably about school and the neighborhood, and finally gave him the annual donation in the colored envelope that the parish sent to our house monthly. My sister and I had little envelopes, too, that we put in the baskets during the weekly collections. They said, "My Offering" on the front, and on the flap, "God will bless you for every offering you make in His name."

Before the priest left, he blessed us in the name of the Father and the Son and the Holy Spirit while we knelt on the living-room carpet by the front door.

I knew that if I crossed myself precisely, the priest's blessing would work, as the nuns said, more efficaciously. It was also important to have the right intent when you prayed, they explained. This was a good thing to know because I believed that God was, among other things, an excellent backup in case I hadn't studied for a test. My parents told my sister and me that education was very important, and so I wanted very much to do well in school. So my childhood prayers ran heavily along the lines of asking God to solve any and all of my problems: Let me get an A on this test. Let me be popular. Let me be better at sports. I prayed to my God, the Great Problem Solver.

As a young boy, I said my prayers each night in front of a plastic glow-in-the-dark picture of the *Pietà* that my grandparents had purchased during a trip to the New York World's Fair in 1964. By the time it reached my dresser, the features of the Madonna and Child were all but obliterated; all that remained was a white fluorescent blob on a navy background. Later, I discovered a picture of the real *Pietà* in one of my mother's heavy art books that she kept in the living-room bookcase. It was only with great imagination that I connected Michelangelo's *Pietà* with the version that helped me to pray.

I also prayed regularly to St. Jude. That he was patron saint of impossible causes made him an immensely practical saint: I would pray to God first, and if God himself couldn't answer my prayer, then *surely* it was an impossible cause. Then I prayed to St. Jude.

Because I liked getting mail, I clipped a notice in a magazine and sent away to the National Shrine of St. Jude in Maryland. For three dollars, they sent me a beige, ten-inch plastic statue of St. Jude and a prayer book with long, complicated prayers. Some were even in Latin. To my mind, the longer prayers were better, and those in Latin were the most efficacious of all. I used the Latin prayers for only the biggest, most important tests. Saint Jude stood patiently on my dresser for a few years until I decided he was doing only a mediocre job of solving my impossible causes and relegated him into my underwear drawer.

I had a pleasantly unremarkable 1960s childhood. It had its painful moments and occasional problems, but I grew up in a good, loving home. I was as happy as any of my pals, and enjoyed good friends and good grades through high school. Perhaps thanks to St. Jude praying for me from inside my dresser drawer.

I worked hard in high school and spent the summers earning money for myself and eventually for college, first cutting lawns and then working as a paperboy, a dishwasher, a waiter, a caddie, a theater usher, a bank teller and, for one miserable summer, on an assembly line putting little boxes into big boxes. Eventually, I thought about college.

In junior year in high school, I made it to the top of my class and did well on the college boards, so I decided to apply to the better colleges. At the time, the only good schools I knew anything about were those in the Ivy League. The idea of looking into other non-Ivy colleges never crossed my mind. As for Catholic colleges, I had as little interest in them as my Jewish friends probably did. The only ones I had even heard of were Georgetown and Notre Dame, and because I knew almost nothing about either (except that Notre Dame was a big football school), I didn't bother sending away for applications. Attending a Catholic college seemed about as sensible as continuing with C.C.D. classes. Who wanted to study religion all the time, anyway? The Ivy League, according to my parents, my guidance counselor, and my friends, was where I needed to go.

By that time, I had also decided to major in business. Granted, I hadn't actually taken any "business" courses in high school (they offered only "bookkeeping") and I considered the F.B.L.A. Club (Future Business Leaders of America) the primary reserve for geeks in our school. And there were many other things that I found infinitely more interesting—art, English, history. But I couldn't imagine making a career out of the things I really liked. What did one *do* with an art degree? Paint? And with an English degree? How could you make a living?

Business therefore was a practical compromise and the perfect solution to my problem. After all, my parents told me, I could get into the "business" end of anything. That seemed sensible, and my guidance counselor heartily agreed.

Many of my friends at the time made similar decisions, rejecting pursuits like literature and fine arts and opting instead for business, because it was more "practical." And who could argue otherwise? Part of the reason was the high cost of a college education. After all, my family did not have much money. I knew I would have a lot of loans to pay off and couldn't imagine paying them off with a career in history or art.

So after applying to a number of places, I decided to attend the University of Pennsylvania, the one Ivy League school that had an undergraduate business program. My parents were doubly happy. It was an excellent school, or so everyone said, and I would be close to home.

THE UNIVERSITY OF Pennsylvania is the oldest university in the country. Harvard, they were fond of pointing out during the campus tours at Penn, is an older *college*. The university is situated on a largely self-contained campus in West Philadelphia. Its buildings are a pleasantly jumbled mixture of Gothic, Jacobean, Colonial, and modern architecture. It is a distinctly urban campus, but with enough trees, flowering bushes, and secluded cobbled walks to keep it from feeling too citified.

When I arrived in 1978, Penn was emerging from a sort of identity crisis. Saddled with a Quaker sense of propriety and modesty, it had neither sought nor gained the cachet of Harvard or Yale or nearby Princeton, its hated rival. While this engendered a more competitive school spirit, it also meant, happily, that there was far less of the snobbery found at the other Ivies. But while it might not have had the reputation of its Ivy brothers, Penn was well known for its graduate schools: the medical school, the law school, the nursing school, the Moore School of Engineering, the Annenberg School of Communication and, particularly, the Wharton School of Business. These graduate schools lent Penn a decided air of professionalism and seriousness, quite different from the liberal arts atmosphere of the other Ivies. All in all, Penn remained surprisingly close to the eminently *practical* vision of an American university as laid out by its founder, Benjamin Franklin, in 1740.

During my freshman year I lived in the Quadrangle, an enormous nineteenth-century enclosure of brick dormitories the size of a few football fields, and decorated with leering gargoyles, mullioned windows, and soaring onion-domed turrets. Immense statues dotted the individual quadrangles—an eighteenth-century preacher, a former provost of the college, and monuments to the Fallen Men of the Great War. It breathed history, and I delighted in passing through the tall iron gates every morning on my way to class (and occasionally being carried through them, drunk, at night). I adored everything about Penn that spoke of tradition: the ancient, gnarled ivy branches that crawled up the sides of the classroom buildings, the immense hundred-year-old trees on College Green, the faded memorials to long-dead graduates. I liked passing under the huge iron gate near Houston Hall with the motto *Inveniemus viam aut faciemus*: We will find a way or we will make a way. The covers of our spiral-bound notebooks were emblazoned with the college seal and motto, *Leges sine moribus vanae*: Laws without morals are useless.

I was also jubilant to have been accepted into Wharton, which was reputed to be the best business school in the country.

And at first, I loved the course work. A new world opened itself up to me: concepts like supply and demand, equity, debt, leverage, futures, capital. It was like learning a new language that unlocked the arcana of the financial pages. The economy and the world at large began to make more sense, and I felt suddenly very adult.

And immediately after I began studying at Wharton came the heady realization of the apparently limitless opportunities that lay ahead. Business students heard daily of the high-powered jobs and tantalizing opportunities awaiting us just on the other side of graduation, the startling starting salaries offered to seniors, the prestigious companies recruiting on campus, the famous Wharton grads and the mountains of money they made. It was exhilarating, especially for a seventeen-year-old.

My fellow Penn students were talented young people—intelligent, inquisitive, and diligent. They were also, particularly at Wharton, almost preternaturally competitive. The difficult business courses required long hours of work in order to master abstruse financial concepts like backward-bending supply curves, accounting for nonconsolidated affiliates, and the marginal propensity to consume. With the exception of the more qualitative courses like management and marketing, the business courses were uniformly grueling. And since everyone else prepared weeks in advance for the midterms and finals, and exams were graded on the curve, I had to study just as diligently to achieve the requisite B. The rare A was a cause for celebration. When I received a C in statistics—my first ever—I felt surprisingly little anger; I had had absolutely *no* idea what the teacher had been talking about for the greater part of the semester.

As a result, I spent most of my nights during freshman year in the bowels of Med School Library, which I preferred for its morgue-like quiet over the university's noisier main library. My friends, I knew, thought me something of a grind. Once, after having failed to convince me to join them drinking on a Thursday night, they grabbed my arms and legs, carried me out of the Quad, and headed for the nearest bar. I struggled for a few minutes and finally decided to relax. As soon as my companions realized I was enjoying the ride, they promptly deposited me on the pavement. I accompanied them the rest of the way on foot.

The tense atmosphere at Wharton served to make already competitive students even more driven, sometimes obsessively so. During the first semester of freshman year, one of our accounting professors scheduled a review session one week before the final exam. I had heard about this and asked another Wharton student for more details.

"When's the review session?" I asked.

"I don't really know," he said airily.

But I was sure that he did, in fact, know. Nevertheless, despite my best efforts, he refused to reveal the time of the review session—apparently because he wanted to maintain an advantage when the finals rolled around. Eventually, I discovered the time and place on my own, and when I walked into the review session I found the other fellow seated in the front row.

Studying at Wharton also meant that my intellectual path grew increasingly more narrow. To do well in business school, other courses (in the liberal arts, for example) needed to be limited. There simply wasn't time for challenging courses in other areas.

To assist us in selecting our courses at Wharton, for example, we were instructed each semester to meet with our faculty advisers. I never saw my almost mythical adviser outside of our twice-yearly ten-minute meeting, which made it difficult for him to "advise" me on anything. He barely could remember my name. Nevertheless, I dutifully trotted off to his office each semester before registration.

In the spring of my freshman year, I mentioned to my adviser that I was thinking of registering for a course in American poetry. His eyes widened, and then narrowed with suspicion.

"Whatever for?" he asked.

"Well," I said, "I thought it might be . . . um . . . interesting."

"I would strongly advise you against taking anything like *that*," he said. "It will only take time away from the important courses. If you take a nonbusiness course, at *least* take an easy one. When interviewing time comes, no one will give a shit about how you did in a poetry course."

Since I rarely took his advice anyway, his warning didn't much concern me. I took the course, received an A, and, as it turned out, remembered far more from that course than any business course.

Freshman year passed quickly, almost in a blur. My choice of courses had been fairly random, since I wasn't required to declare on a major until sophomore year. More important than the studies, though, was the heady adventure of being on my own, away from my family. And I returned home that summer full of the cynicism and snideness that can be learned only at the country's better schools. I could only begin to gauge how officious I sounded from the looks on my family's faces as I revealed to them the Many Truths I had learned during freshman year.

A few years later, when Carolyn returned from her own freshman year at Harvard and demonstrated the same attitudes over one Thanksgiving dinner, I asked my parents, "Was I this bad?"

"Oh," my father laughed. "Much worse."

One result of this heightened regard for my own intellect was that I engaged more frequently with my college friends in debates about religion. While I still possessed only a ten-year-old's understanding of Catholicism, this happy ignorance didn't prevent me from arguing continually with my friend George, a confirmed agnostic, about almost any religious topic: Did Jesus really perform miracles? What's the point of organized religion? Did Jesus rise from the dead? What's the point of confession if God knows all your sins? Is there a God?

But while this arguing may have helped to hone my understanding of religion, it also served largely to inoculate me against any sort of real relationship with God. While there was clear passion in our debates, it was the dry, formal passion of the intellect: George and I might as easily have been arguing politics or economics. Indeed, any religious concepts that I couldn't comprehend were quickly dismissed. And anything that couldn't be proven rationally I deemed meaningless or silly.

For the most part, then, outside of those late-night debates, religion was ignored within my circle of friends. It's not that my new friends were not decent and moral people. Rather, organized religion was simply foreign to us. During my senior year, I watched the series *Brideshead Revisited* on PBS along with some friends, and heard Evelyn Waugh's alter ego, Charles Ryder, express very neatly his own attitude towards religion:

> The view implicit in my education was that the basic narrative of Christianity had long been exposed as a myth, and that opinion was now divided as to whether its ethical teaching was of present value, a division in which the main weight went against it; religion was a hobby which some people professed and others did not; at the best it was slightly ornamental, at worst it was the province of "complexes" and "inhibitions"—catch-words of the decade—and of the intolerance, hypocrisy and sheer stupidity attributed to it for centuries.

That sounded about right.

I STILL WENT to Mass, though. And why not? I felt content sitting in church, if only for its comforting ritual. The Mass was solid, enduring, familiar.

More to the point, it certainly couldn't hurt. If there *were* a God, I could perhaps placate him by going to church, especially if I was planning on asking him for anything. You never know, to paraphrase Pascal's famous wager.

So I frequented a small church in the neighborhood, St. Agatha-St. James. Early on, I had experimented with the university's campus ministry at the Newman Center along with Bruce, one of my few semipracticing Catholic friends. One

Sunday, we went to Mass at the Newman Center chapel—a large meeting hall illuminated by fluorescent lights and furnished with grey metal chairs that faced a sort of high table that served as the altar. The words of the day's entrance hymn were projected on the white cinder-block wall behind the altar. As we sang "Gift of Finest Wheat," a scruffy young priest wearing sandals walked in and started chatting with us before the Mass. Students helped to distribute Communion. We talked about what the gospel reading meant to us. At the "Our Father," the priest asked us to hold hands. Whatever this was, I thought, it was not church. The following Sunday, Bruce and I returned to the backwards, but more comfortable, local parish.

We particularly enjoyed the sermons at St. Agatha's. One Sunday we sat in the pew after the gospel reading, chatting, and not paying any particular attention to the proceedings. At one point during his homily, the priest remarked, "God wants us to get the most out of any situation in life."

Then this: "Yes, God wants us to ask ourselves of everything in life: What's in this for *me*? God wants us to say, 'What's in this for *me*?'"

Bruce smiled and whispered archly, "Now *that's* a religion I can live with."

So I remained a cultural Catholic during college, adhering to the rules of the Church without understanding much of its spirit. In my junior year, however, I ran into real religion, or at the very least, real faith.

On Memorial Day, a few weeks after the semester had ended, a good friend and former roommate, Brad, was killed in an automobile accident along with the girlfriend of another friend. Both were twenty years old.

Brad had been my freshman-year roommate. He got me drunk for the first time in my life, taught me the proper way to roll a joint, took me to my first foreign film, introduced me to an astonishing number of drinking games, and instructed me on the correct way to dress at Penn—that is, topsiders, khaki pants, and Oxford-cloth button-down shirts. ("No unnatural fibers; no colors not found in nature," he said, when I asked what he wanted for his birthday.) We played practical jokes on our hallmates and, more frequently, on each other. I had spent weekends with his family, knew his girlfriend(s), his plans for the future, and was, one afternoon, caught with him in a surprise thunderstorm miles from campus; we simply took off our shoes and walked back to the dorm, laughing. He was a wonderful friend.

Since the accident happened over the Memorial Day weekend, most of us had already returned home for summer break. The bad news was relayed by phone, very quickly, from one to another. Brad was buried on a very muggy morning, a few days later, in Washington, D.C.

During the service, listening to the minister talk about God's love and mercy, I made the decision not to go to church any longer. I decided quickly and clearly. As far as I could see, there could be no rational explanation for a loving God who could do something like this. So why bother with the charade of religion?

A few months later, after returning to Penn for my senior year, I was chatting with Jacque, a shy, quiet girl in our circle of friends. Jacque, who had lived in our hall freshman year, was from a small town outside of Chicago and was what we called a "fundamentalist" (although I doubt that any of us knew what this meant at the time). She attended "Bible study groups" and took the time to "find" the right church at which to worship.

Brad and Jacque, in many ways opposites, were nevertheless close friends. Brad was wild and energetic; Jacque was, well, a "fundamentalist." But there was ample room for misfits (or so I imagine they must have thought of each other) in their lives.

So one cold, clear day near the end of November, I stood shivering outside the Quad and told Jacque how angry I was at God for having taken Brad away, and how I had not gone to church since he died. And I think I was angry at *her*, too, for believing in a God who could do something like this. I was looking for an intellectual answer from her that would respond to my anger and frustration. I suppose she realized that I was, in a way, challenging her.

She closed her eyes for a few seconds, opened them again, and said, "Well, I've been praying to God and thanking him for Brad's life."

Hearing this, I felt a change, a subtle shift inside me. Instead of the intellectual, almost mathematical, answer I had sought, Jacque gave me the briefest glimpse of a new way of looking at things. A small thing perhaps, but I began to see the difference between faith and reason, between the intellect and the soul—and between my world and hers. So I figured I'd give God another chance and go back to church.

MY SENIOR YEAR continued without incident; and our classes grew progressively more challenging as we moved beyond the intro stuff and into advanced accounting and finance courses. By now, the finance courses had become almost entirely quantitative, with complicated equations and graphs designed to explicate the often mind-bending economic theories. Still, I enjoyed the challenge and felt like I was learning important, real-world skills.

Even though I had decided to be a finance major, I decided to sign up for additional accounting courses to bolster my résumé. But intermediate accounting required an enormous amount of work, and exams came to us on sixteen legal-sized sheets filled with income statements and balance sheets. "The test will be four hours long," our accounting instructor would announce. "You have two hours to do it." Although I seemed completely unable to get anything above a B, I still looked forward to those plum, high-paying jobs.

But for now, despite my summer jobs and loans and work-study jobs, I needed to earn extra money. By my senior year, I was so strapped for cash that I volunteered for experiments at the Department of Psychology. The department paid students five dollars an hour to participate in their experiments, an excellent wage at the time. I got the idea from Bruce, who volunteered not only for psych tests but also for medical tests to earn extra pocket money. One time he showed up with rows of strange-looking metal disks taped to his arm. "Dermatology tests," he explained. "They pay five bucks a disk!"

Most of the psychological tests consisted of Rorschach blots and simple question-and-answer sessions, although one involved gazing at small pictures of animals on pieces of white cardboard. Your head was supposed remain immobile while a grad student slowly moved the pictures in and out of your range of vision. I got a headache along with the ten dollars.

Bruce and I soon discovered that the more bizarre were our answers on the tests, the better were our chances of being called back for another five-dollar session. So we concocted what we imagined were answers that a deranged person might say.

By the end of the semester, we were especially proficient at the "general intelligence" section, since most of the tests included the same questions. Eventually, we wrote down the questions from memory and even spent time tracking down the answers in an encyclopedia. "When was Goethe born?" "How far is it from Los Angeles to New York?" "Where does rubber come from?" After memorizing the correct responses, we parroted them back during the exams. Undoubtedly, we scored very high on general intelligence. As a result of our zeal (and desire to cash in), the examiners probably concluded that their "random" sample indicated that Penn seniors were severely maladjusted but highly intelligent.

As graduation approached, I grew increasingly confused about the future. Part of me wanted to continue with business; I had obviously invested enough time in my studies. During my last summer before graduation, I had even worked in a stock brokerage in Philadelphia and had enjoyed finally putting some of my education to use.

Still, I had my doubts. Business, although interesting, was certainly not what I considered fun (accounting in particular). I was astonished that some of my friends at Wharton actually *liked* reading magazines like *Fortune* and *Business Week*, both of which I found unspeakably dull. Maybe I could do something else. But what? What could I do to support myself? I had taken a business law course and enjoyed that. Perhaps law school. But this was out of the question: I had no money for graduate school.

When I admitted this confusion, my friends responded the same way: "Why did you go to Wharton if you weren't going to get a job in business?" Everyone told me how fortunate I was even to *be* at Wharton with such a promising career path in front of me: the "fast track," as we called it, to success. With a finance degree I was pretty much guaranteed a great starting salary. How could you *not* go into business? they asked. Some of the investment banks were even offering $25,000 to undergrads. So when the time came, I dutifully signed up for interviews with the investment banks, corporations, commercial banks, and consulting groups that annually flocked to Penn.

Interviewing proved tremendously diverting. For one thing, I received stacks of mail. For another, Wharton made the whole process almost embarrassingly simple. In point of fact, when "interviewing season" (also known as fall) arrived, I did almost nothing but write a résumé. The Career Planning & Placement Department boasted an entire wall of bulletin boards on which were posted descriptions of dozens of juicy jobs—new ones every week.

The "Big Eight" public accounting firms arrived first, to skim off the cream of the accounting students. Within a few weeks, there came a noticeable lull in senior accounting classes as students who had accepted job offers suddenly lost all interest in grades. Next came the investment banks and brokerage houses—Salomon Brothers, Lehman Brothers, Goldman Sachs, Smith Barney, Merrill Lynch—on the prowl for finance majors. Finally, in a frenzy of activity in mid-November came the big "money-center banks" like Chase Manhattan, Citicorp, Manufacturers Hanover; large industrial corporations like IBM, AT&T and GE; as well as elite management consulting agencies like Booz Allen and Boston Consulting Group.

To sign up for an interview, the job-hungry senior simply needed to drop a typeset résumé into one of a number of mailbox slots on the wall. Next to each slot was a 3 x 5 inch card with the company's name and a short job description. Career Planning then forwarded your résumé to the corresponding company. Then, as if by magic, in a few days you would be invited to an interview on campus. You would wear a Brooks Brothers three-piece suit (navy), an Oxford-cloth button-down shirt (white—or pale blue for the adventurous), and a silk rep tie (Penn's red and blue was preferable). Women wore the identical outfit, except for a skirt and a floppy silk foulard bow. A trench coat was also required, to be slung casually over your arm. One friend spied me marching purposefully across campus on a warm September day with an obviously superfluous overcoat. She asked me if I couldn't have just bought a fake folded coat, since it was more like a prop than a real coat. I laughed, but felt unmasked. It *was* a prop, and I felt like an actor auditioning for an unfamiliar role.

Most of the interviews were easy and fun. There was little preparation needed, save for perusing the occasional annual report. The companies were anxious to sign us on, and it was flattering to be wooed. Larger companies, especially the Big Eight accounting firms, even hosted late-afternoon cocktail parties in hotels near campus. Free food! But after a few months of answering the same canned interview questions, discussing your academic background *ad nauseam*, and struggling to convince someone why having been student council president in high school meant that I would be a stellar mortgage banker, the attraction began to wane.

But some of the interviews—particularly with the investment banks—were actually painful.

In the early 1980s, investment banks were the most popular places for undergraduates, for one compelling reason: they paid the most money. (Wharton students joked that the honest answer to the question, "Why are you interested in working for us?" was "Because you're hiring.")

While most interviews were scheduled after the companies had screened résumés and selected candidates, Salomon Brothers, a large investment bank, arranged their interviews on a first-come, first-served basis. We suspected this served to weed out the merely curious, leaving only those most desperate to work as investment bankers. Which was, of course, precisely what Salomon was looking for.

The line for the Salomon Brothers' sign-up sheet formed at 6 A.M., when dozens of caffeinated seniors dutifully lined up outside the Career Planning office. Despite my interest in both investment banking and making pots of money, I was not about to rise at 6 A.M. for *anything*, so I wandered over to the office around 9:00, before my first class. Miraculously, I snagged one of the last spots after someone scratched her name off.

The next week, as I waited in the reception area at Career Planning, I was greeted by a tall, blond-haired fellow dressed exactly like me (although I suspected that he owned more suits than the one he was wearing and that his cashmere topcoat was definitely *not* a prop).

He led me into a small, windowless room with a round table and three chairs. He sat down, looked at me, and said "Uhhh . . . "

He glanced down at my résumé. "Jim!" he exclaimed, apparently happy to get my name right.

"Right," he said to himself. "Yeah. Now, where else are you interviewing?"

"Oh," I said casually, "a few other investment banks, corporate finance departments, and some commercial banks."

His left eyebrow rose. "Commercial banks?" he inquired. By his tone of voice, I might just as well have said that I was interviewing with Ringling Brothers for a job as a performing seal. "*Commercial* banks?" The second time he practically spat out the words.

"Do you know the difference between an investment bank like Salomon Brothers and a commercial bank?" he asked. "I certainly *hope* you know the difference between a commercial bank and an investment bank."

Now, asking a question like this to a finance major is something like asking a baseball player if he understands the difference between a ball and a bat.

"Uh, yeah," I said, trying not to sound overly surprised or offended.

"Well . . . what is it?"

I briefly explained the difference. He stared at me.

"Uh huh," he said.

There was a knock on the door. This was rather unusual, as we were in a room reserved exclusively for interviews; interruptions were more or less forbidden. In strode another tall, blond investment banker for Aryan Brothers. He smiled at me.

"Hello, Jim."

"Uh, hi," I said, and then added thoughtfully, "How do you do?"

"Jim," said Aryan #1, "this is Bill."

"Bill," he said to his partner, "Jim here was just telling me that he's interviewing with commercial banks."

Bill looked at me, horrified, "*Commercial* banks?"

The interview went swiftly downhill, and I was ushered out. Later in the day, I learned from other students who had interviewed what I *should* have said. That is: from my earliest childhood memories, I've wanted to work for only Salomon Brothers. Considering something as heretical as, say, working for Chase Manhattan, was simply not good form. I received my rejection letter a few days later.

The opposite was my interview with Wachovia Bank in Winston-Salem. I had slid my résumé in the "Wachovia" slot since I lusted after their opening for a security analyst—helping them choose stocks for their investment portfolio. However, not only had I never heard of Wachovia, I also had little or no inclination of moving to North Carolina.

But my first interview with the friendly Wachovia representative was so enjoyable—the interviewer actually laughed!—that I readily agreed to a second one at their corporate headquarters in North Carolina.

Winston-Salem was a pleasant town built, I later discovered, primarily on tobacco money. (That I didn't realize this fact from the town's name shows how little research I was

doing for my interviews.) Wachovia's headquarters were
located in the tallest building of a town that seemed populated
entirely by transplanted Northerners. Everyone I met was
remarkably friendly, and the job sounded terrific.
The bank was planning to hire only one security analyst
that year, and it seemed that they wanted me. They made quite
a pitch. A cheerful woman from personnel drove me around
Winston-Salem and gave me an extended tour. At the end of our
drive she pulled in front of a cozy-looking white clapboard
house with a wrap-around porch. Wachovia had already
selected an apartment for me, she said, subject to my approval.
It was an enormous, sunny apartment, the first floor of this
bright, airy house, with a large yard. Fully furnished, it rented
for about $300 per month. I liked the friendly people at
Wachovia, liked the job, and rapidly calculated that, on this
salary, I would be able to save a lot of money very quickly.

"And," she said, "since we know that you'll probably have
a lot of unforeseen expenses like furniture, clothes, things like
that, we'll give you an extra $2,000." Not bad. On the other
hand, Winston-Salem seemed pretty sleepy; it didn't seem there
would be much to do after work.

A few days after the trip to North Carolina, I had an interview with General Electric. G.E. ran a high-powered financial
training program for recent college grads that was reputed to be
the best in corporate America. After a nod for a second interview, G.E. asked me to select three possible locations. I filled
out their questionnaire and listed my choices: Philadelphia
(G.E. Aerospace, their peaceable name for military defense
systems), New York (G.E. International), and Washington, D.C.
(G.E. Information Systems, their new computer division).

For some reason, I was asked to fly to none of these locales
but, instead, to Lynn, Massachusetts, for the second interview.
Lynn was the headquarters of G.E. Aircraft Engines, an
immense plant comprised of dozens of old factory buildings.
Their aircraft engine business, which had boomed during the
Second World War, had fallen off considerably since then, and
many of the buildings were now empty. To reach the finance

office, I was led through an open, noisy factory floor—a decidedly different experience than being shown around a tony accounting firm where there were no forklifts to dodge on my way to interviews. But they actually *made* something here. I liked that. It made their business easier to appreciate.

On the other hand, the offices were cramped, mean, cinderblock affairs, painted in a grammar-school lime green. During my interview, I found myself daydreaming about Wachovia and my sunny $300 apartment in Winston-Salem.

At noon, I met with three Financial Management Program trainees who tried to convince me to work at Lynn. They knew that I hadn't requested that location but gave it a shot nonetheless. On the drive to lunch, I asked what it was like to live in Lynn. There wasn't a whole lot to do, one said, but the town was "coming back." The city had just embarked on an urban renewal program that focused on one particular block. Then the three of them looked at each other and burst out laughing. "Unfortunately, it just burned down!" blurted one. Indeed, a few minutes later we passed an entire block of still-smoldering brick buildings. It did not inspire much confidence in Lynn's renaissance. I hoped I wouldn't end up here.

After a round of second interviews with a variety of companies, corporate hiring officers began contacting me on a regular basis. Some would send what we called "love notes" reminding us how wonderful their company was, how extensive their benefits were, and how much they were looking forward to welcoming us to the "Arthur Andersen team," the "Wachovia team," or the "G.E. family." Wachovia's senior vice president called me on Saturday morning at 8:00 (had he ever gone to college? I wondered) to tell me how much he wanted me on his team.

I was barely awake, and by the time I had realized who it was the conversation was over. "Great talking with you, pal!"

Before I fell back asleep, I briefly wondered what I had said.

Eventually, I narrowed down the offers to General Electric and Arthur Andersen, the public accounting firm that offered a training position in their management consulting department in either Chicago or Washington, D.C. As friendly and encouraging as they were at Wachovia, I just couldn't see moving to Winston-Salem. When I sent Wachovia a polite "no," they graciously called me to say that if things didn't work out at G.E. or Arthur Andersen, I would always be welcome at Wachovia.

During my final conversation with G.E., I told the interviewer that I was seriously considering working for Arthur Andersen. (By now, I knew enough not to tell him about commercial banks.)

"Well," said the interviewer, "it's really not a difficult choice."

"It's not?" I said.

"Jim," he chuckled slightly. "Do you know what they will write on your tombstone if you work for Arthur Andersen?"

"No. What?"

"Your tombstone will say: *Here lies Jim Martin. He worked for Arthur Andersen.* Period!"

He paused dramatically. "Because that's *all* you'll have time for!"

I certainly didn't want *that* to happen. He seemed to be implying that I wouldn't be working quite so many hours at G.E. And that was good enough for me. I didn't want to kill myself for Arthur Andersen, and G.E. seemed like a good deal. The training program sounded interesting—two years of six-month job rotations. And, as it turned out, it looked like I could even get a placement in New York. One of my college friends, Rob, had just accepted with an accounting firm in New York, so I also knew I'd have a good roommate.

But what really convinced me was the money: $20,000 a year. I calculated what my take-home pay would be, grinned, and said yes.

2.

Petals on a Bough

The apparition of these faces in the crowd;
Petals on a wet, black bough.

Ezra Pound, "In a Station of the Metro"

In 1982, General Electric was revving up for the Age of Greed. Its chief executive officer, John F. Welch, who had taken over in 1981, had informed G.E.'s businesses (G.E. was large enough that each of its individual divisions was called and indeed *was* a separate "businesses") that if a business were not No. 1 or 2 in its industry, it would be sold or closed. Or, in G.E. lingo, "Move up or Move out."

The businesses' response was "downsizing," a concept much in vogue at the time. Corporate America was thought to be heavy with too many unnecessary midlevel managers. In theory, the superfluous layers of management slowed companies down and gobbled up funds that could have been used more profitably for things like research and development. CEOs, then, needed to cut heads. G.E. took the lead in this area.

As a result, Mr. Welch, to his evident chagrin, earned the nickname "Neutron Jack." Like the recently developed neutron bomb, it was said that after Mr. Welch had visited a G.E. facility the buildings were left standing but the people were gone. In the *Wall Street Journal* and the business magazines, though,

Mr. Welch was touted as the vanguard of the new, high-powered 1980's CEO who would make his company "lean and mean." Just how lean and mean I would find out later.

On the other hand, Welch's predecessor as CEO, Reginald Jones, was an executive of the old school: courtly and polished—a gentleman. And while Jack Welch may not have commanded the same degree of loyalty from his employees, his impact on G.E.'s bottom line also earned him the adoration of Wall Street and the business schools. In a few years, Welch would essentially transform General Electric from a stodgy blue-chip company to a trendsetting international corporate powerhouse.

So naturally I was elated to have landed the job with G.E. The possibilities for advancement were almost limitless— General Electric was gargantuan; they had so many different divisions that you could work in almost any type of industry, in any capacity. The salaries and benefits packages were excellent: employees called it "Generous Electric." And the training program I entered was reputed to be almost as good an M.B.A. program. I knew that if I did well, I could go far and make pots of money.

The International Division was located in the G.E. building on 51st Street and Lexington Avenue in midtown Manhattan. The 1933 art deco structure, rising over the low dome of St. Bartholomew's Church on Park Avenue, is a slim brick building topped by a four-story crown of lightning bolts, radio waves, and other fanciful architectural decorations. It is next to the Waldorf-Astoria and two blocks away from St. Patrick's Cathedral and Saks Fifth Avenue. In the summer, you could sit in the broad plaza in front of the Seagram's Building, listen to the lunchtime bands, eat Greek food from sidewalk vendors, and watch the milling corporate crowds.

The building's interior was something of a disappointment, though, not as posh as some of the midtown offices that housed my investment banker friends. While G.E. was trying assiduously to shed its stodgy image as a mere "manufacturer," it nevertheless clung tenaciously to the idea that money should be spent on the product, not on the office. As a result, 570 Lexington, while clean and freshly painted, was filled with junky grey-metal file cabinets, ancient telephones, and torn boxes of accounting records.

On my first day, I put on my best grey suit (actually my *only* grey suit) and a new tie that I had bought the day before at Brooks Brothers on Madison Avenue. The coordinator of the Financial Management Program, a balding, young, blond-haired fellow named Sandy, met me in the lobby and led me to his comfortable office on the twenty-first floor. Sandy worked in Financial Planning and Analysis with a person improbably named "Rusty" Nail, because of his red hair. I looked around Sandy's office, admiring the comfy red leather chair behind his desk, his personal computer, the expensive prints on the wall, the framed photos on his desk. He told me he was happy I was starting. Me too, I said. My first "rotation," he explained, would be working in the Income Margin Department, where I would, not surprisingly, look after "margins." Was that okay? he asked. Sure.

I spent a few hours plowing through G.E. benefits marginalia. Did I want to participate in the company's Savings and Security Program where I could have money withdrawn from my paycheck and matched by the company? Yes. Did I understand that as a part of the agreement I couldn't withdraw the money for three years? Yes. Did I want my check to be directly deposited in a bank in New York? I didn't even know they could do that, but okay. Would I sign a paper saying that I would abide by the ethical rules of the company? I read quickly and signed an agreement saying that I wouldn't divulge company secrets and that I would act "ethically." Did anyone notice my new Brooks Brothers tie? I wondered.

Two G.E. trainees took me to a restaurant called Bun 'n' Brew for lunch. Thanks to my expensive college education, I was now a superbly accomplished drinker, and the three of us consumed two pitchers of beer. After an hour, we emerged from the Bun 'n' Brew onto the crowded, fetid streets of Manhattan. I felt an immediate desire both to sleep and urinate.

We returned to the office, and I realized that I had drunk far too much—on my first day of work, the day for which I had prepared for the past four years. Horrified, I rushed to the bathroom and rinsed out my mouth to hide the insidious smell of beer. I feared that, were my secret revealed, I would be fired on the spot, still naïvely unaware that drinking at lunch was far from a major offense.

My job in Income Margin consisted of reporting the profit earned by our business groups. Our office tracked the profitability of various projects across the world that used G.E. products—gas turbine engines, power generators—which at the time all seemed to be in Saudi Arabia. Most of the work was straight accounting—reams and reams of journal entries on carbon sheets, financial reports, and account reconciliations that were Xeroxed and sent to scores of executives. My main task was to complete a long monthly report full of dozens of columns of numbers. Personal computers wouldn't be available to the trainees for another year or so, so I was nervous about not making any mistakes on the long twelve-column green spreadsheets.

Trainees were also expected to take two years of in-house accounting and finance courses that ran during the fall and spring. Since we had the summers off, it was easy to feel like I was still on an academic calendar. The dull Monday afternoon classes, focusing on arcane General Electric accounting practices and procedures, were taught by the division's managers. Our salary increases and our next job rotation depended not only on our job performance but also on our grades, so competition in class was especially fierce. But after Wharton, this was old hat. Still, I was annoyed to realize that it meant another two years of studying at nights and on the weekends.

I remembered the comment from the G.E. interviewer about my tombstone epitaph and working too much overtime, and repeated it to one of my bosses. "God, who told you that bullshit?" she said. My new roommate, Rob, said I was the only person who had studied accounting at Wharton so he could get a job where he studied accounting.

Happily, I had a wonderful manager—a good-natured woman named Marge who had worked for G.E. for many years. Marge was a Brooklynite who took a relaxed attitude towards life, and she made life at G.E. enjoyable and human. We had fun chatting while we worked, and she took nothing (including the work) too seriously.

Along with Marge I worked with Louise, a longtime G.E. employee and, incidentally, a great admirer of Elvis Presley. Louise kept a framed picture of The King in her office, and each year, on the anniversary of Elvis's death, she showed up in a black dress and black earrings. After lunch, she served a black cake (dark chocolate, as it turned out) for the office, while "Love Me Tender" played continuously on a cassette player. I was introduced to this tradition my first month at work and was amazed not so much by her custom, but that everyone else seemed quite unfazed by it. "I love Elvis Day," said Marge, after we had polished off the cake. Likewise, on non-Elvis Days, when one of Elvis's songs came on the radio, Louise would ask everyone in the office to stop talking. This included, at least for Louise, phone conversations. If Louise was speaking on the phone, she would suddenly tell the caller that she had to go.

Louise worked with Sherry, who had a similar affection for Frank Sinatra. (We were, however, permitted to talk during Frank's songs.) When Sherry was hired by G.E. in the 1960s, her coworkers suggested that she not inform the management that she was married. (Managers were then of the opinion that single women made more dedicated workers.) So Sherry remained officially "single" and, although she had worked for G.E. for thirty years and although her daughter visited the office regularly, Sherry still referred to her husband as her "brother" and her daughter as her "niece." Everyone in the office did likewise, to be polite.

The twenty or so young trainees spent a lot of time together, dancing at the clubs in Manhattan, throwing parties in our apartments, going to movies, and—especially—hanging out at nearby bars, where there were plenty of free munchies during happy hour. During the summer, there were free concerts in Central Park, cheap baseball games at Shea or Yankee Stadium, and the occasional Broadway show. Most social events were followed by a visit to a bar on the Upper East Side. And as often as not, there was cocaine in the bathroom for the adventurous, compliments of whomever was flush with cash.

My favorite new perk was hosting college recruits for interview lunches on a G.E. expense account—the ultimate luxury, as far as I was concerned. Two trainees were assigned by management to accompany the college recruits to lunch and answer their questions. It was ostensibly a time for the recruits to "relax," but we filled out evaluations of them after the lunch anyway. The official limit for a meal for three people was $100 and, among the trainees, the measure of a successful lunch was how close one came to that mark. It was also a marked relief to be on the other side of the interviewing table, with a job, instead of looking for one.

New York, for me at age twenty-one, was perfect. I drew energy from the pace, the crowds, the noise, and the feeling that I was in the middle of everything that mattered. Discovering the newest restaurants, the most outrageous dance clubs, the hottest Broadway shows, and the latest movies became part of the adventure of living in New York. On the weekends, I went to the Frick Museum just a few blocks from my apartment, the Museum of Modern Art, the Morgan Library, or the Metropolitan Museum, where no matter how many times I went, I always saw something new. It was easy to get a bit spoiled, slightly self-contained, and utterly self-satisfied. At one point, I ran across John Updike's observation that New Yorkers think that people who live anywhere else in the country are "kidding." Which sounded about right.

Six months after I started at G.E., I received the first of the frequent raises that accrued to trainees, and my bank account started to swell accordingly. It was a new experience to treat my friends to an expensive meal and, likewise, to forget a few minutes later how much I had spent. Or to buy a fistful of beautiful silk ties that struck my fancy at Brooks Brothers. The security of having a job with G.E., a decent salary, and an apartment in Manhattan was, at the time, immensely satisfying.

My career at G.E., as it turned out, neatly coincided with the era of Reaganomics and the Age of the Yuppie. Enrollment at undergraduate and graduate business programs soared, and the yuppies produced by the schools poured into jobs at multinational corporations, investment banks, and (even) commercial banks. Although most of my friends and I assiduously avoided the "yuppie" label, there was no denying the fact that, in the early 1980s, we were all very young, certainly urban, and more or less professional. And secretly, I enjoyed a tag that made me feel plugged into the Zeitgeist.

THE MANAGERS at General Electric doted unashamedly on the trainees, constantly reminding us how lucky we were to be G.E. employees: we were part of the "team." At the same time, though, I discovered that, despite the colorful G.E. recruiting brochures with cheerful trainees beaming enthusiastically to their avuncular managers, G.E. was less collegial than I had expected.

As I said, the primary task of my first job was to issue very long, monthly statistical reports. The first month, I informed one executive that our results were coming in low, we probably weren't going to "make our numbers," a cardinal sin. Our contracts in Saudi Arabia that month, I explained, had lost money. "So what?" he said. "Just reverse a few journal entries."

"But that doesn't really represent what we earned," I said, full of four years of accounting beans.

"Listen," he said implacably, "each month we will put out a report and hit the right numbers or we'll get shit from Corporate. So just do whatever it takes to make those numbers."

This meant reversing our reserve accounts every month. In other words, there were sizable reserves—money—squirreled away in miscellaneous accounts that existed for the purpose of allowing us to "make" our monthly target numbers. If we failed to earn sufficient profit on one project, we would simply take it from the reserves of another project. If we made too *much*, we did the opposite, moving money back into the reserve accounts. As a result, we never accurately reported how much money the individual projects actually made. Instead, we showed corporate headquarters what they wanted to see.

Our reserve accounts even had their own names in the ledgers. But while our actual projects would be called, say, "Saudi" and "Turbine," our made-up reserve accounts had names like "Plug" and "Excess" and "Reserve."

This, to put it mildly, seemed less than helpful for corporate headquarters. What was the point of reporting something if you reported only what your superiors wanted to see? How would they know how well the division was doing? It seemed faintly disreputable and certainly poor accounting. The following month, the same executive came into our office and screamed that we hadn't hit the right figures. We needed to reverse more of the reserves. (The target number was usually offered to us at the very last minute.)

Frustrated, I said, "Why should we wait to put out the report at the end of the month? If we know all our figures now, why not just do twelve months of reports?" He stormed out of the office without saying a word.

Louise laughed and said, "You're taking those accounting courses way too seriously."

Besides these new accounting practices, in January of that first year I was introduced to G.E.'s annual closing, the all-encompassing totaling of accounts, and an arduous time for accounting and finance workers. G.E. prided itself on being the first of the major corporations to publish its annual earnings. (Apparently this demonstrated that G.E.'s accountants were speedier than everyone else's.) As a result, there was a frantic rush at the year end to spew out hundreds of financial reports, resulting in the "Final Ledger." Then the "Final Ledger" was revised with correcting journal entries. That gave us the "Final Final Ledger." That one was revised, too. The official name of the year-end ledger was the "Final Final Final Ledger."

All of this necessitated so much overtime that G.E. announced that during the three-week annual closing, employees would not need to go home. Instead, the company reserved rooms in a nearby Manhattan hotel for every employee in the department. Fortunately, I could still commute to my apartment uptown for most of annual closing, but during the last week, when we worked until midnight, I checked into the hotel.

Though we were next door to the Waldorf-Astoria, G.E. reserved us rooms at the decidedly less opulent Summit Hotel across the street, where homeless men wandered bleary-eyed through the airless lobby throughout the night. Towards the end of annual closing that first year, one of the accounting staff, named Cathy, returned to her room one night around 11:00, opened her closet door, looked down, and noticed an extra pair of shoes in the closet. Suddenly a man leapt out, grabbed Cathy and, putting his hand over her mouth, tied her to a chair. At one point he left the room, and Cathy escaped. Cathy said that she had purposely kept her hands loose as she was being tied up. (She had seen that once in a movie, she explained.) Terrified, she made it to the hotel lobby, ran across Lexington Avenue in the slushy snow and into the lobby of the G.E. building, where a few of us returning from a late dinner found her, hysterical. We phoned her brother, who lived with Cathy in the Bronx. He arrived an hour later spouting obscenities about G.E., and drove Cathy home.

When Cathy failed to return to work after a few weeks, the managers informed us that she was recuperating. Finally, one of our managers announced that Cathy was "unbalanced," no longer fit to work at General Electric. Besides, he added, Cathy had never been a dedicated employee, not part of the "team." She did not return.

In January I moved to a new trainee rotation. The job included a spacious office on the fifteenth floor, overlooking Park Avenue, above the beautiful dome of St. Bartholomew's Church, one of the few unobstructed views of Park Avenue. I worked for one of the company's smaller international affiliates—this one based in Italy—managing their sizeable cash accounts, moving money from bank to bank, and totaling and reconciling their accounts. This meant, among other things, that I regularly made large wire transfers over the phone. Eventually, the representatives at Citibank recognized my voice so that I could pick up the phone and have millions of dollars transferred to any account numbers I named.

By the time I began this assignment, I was settled in New York and figured I would stay at G.E. as long as I possibly could. I was relatively content with my job—though I didn't much enjoy the studying—and was having enormous fun with my friends in New York. Rob turned out to be the perfect roommate, a relaxed guy with a sense of humor who never left dishes in the sink. We threw frequent parties in our cramped apartment, bringing together our different circles of friends. One benefit, I quickly learned, of living in Manhattan was the opportunity to meet people far, far outside your normal social circle. A friend at G.E. knew somebody who was in publishing who knew a struggling actor who knew a grad student at Columbia who knew someone working for the U.N. Parties and dinners were invariably eclectic.

Our tiny apartment, though, was not a good place to entertain, especially in the wilting summer heat. During our first standing-room-only party one guest remarked that if we only had straps on the ceiling, it would be exactly like riding in an un-air-conditioned subway car. Indeed, before we got our small, and largely useless, G.E. air conditioner, our apartment was intolerable; I dreaded putting on a suit and tie each morning. One coworker suggested putting underwear in the freezer at night to cool me off in the morning. It sounded kinky but it proved surprisingly effective. The refreshing cool wore off just as I reached the office. The practice stopped, however, when Rob told me that he didn't appreciate finding a plastic bag with my jockey shorts (albeit clean) sitting on top of his Haagen Däzs cartons.

As I moved through the training program, the course work became progressively more difficult and the rotations grew more challenging, requiring ever more overtime. (I kept remembering that tombstone remark from the interview.) And with all the work and studying, I found I had increasingly less free time. Weekends I still tried to keep for myself. Rob enjoyed seeing movies as much as I did and, for some solitude, I would go to the museums.

The best museum for escaping the stress was The Cloisters, the Met's collection of medieval art on the northernmost end of Manhattan, though it was a long subway ride away. In 1936, after picking his way through some abandoned monasteries in Western Europe, John D. Rockefeller assembled his own *faux* monastery to house the Met's immense collection of medieval art. As a result, The Cloisters is crammed with exquisite paintings, sculptures, and stained glass windows, and its small jewel-like gardens are silent but for the occasional passing jet. It was easy to imagine that I was somewhere other than Manhattan as I sat in the quiet, green cloister surrounded by fragrant flowering trees and singing birds.

Visiting churches was another way I tried to break from an increasingly stressed life at work. Taking a whiff of the incense and saying an occasional prayer helped me experience if not interior peace, at least a few minutes of quiet. I stared at the faded paintings and tried to identify the statues of unfamiliar saints. I still prayed, though it was still the kind of prayer that got me through high school and college—to God the Great Problem Solver. But now it was a new set of problems: Let me get a good rotation. Let me get a big raise.

After shopping around for a few months for a decent church in the neighborhood, I settled on St. Vincent Ferrer at 67th Street, run by the Dominican Fathers. It had the three things I was looking for: plenty of stained glass, a good choir, and short homilies. They had numerous parish "activities," too, though I had no time or interest for anything like that. It was enough charity to toss five dollars into the collection basket. And since I noticed that most people gave only one dollar, I considered myself generous.

I even took pride, like some New Yorkers, in stepping over the homeless men and women who would regularly accost me on the street. An out-of-town friend visiting saw me do just that to a man on the pavement who had asked for money.

"How can you do that?" he asked quietly.

"Oh, you get used to it," I said, proud of my urbanity.

On my last rotation, I worked for a department that accounted for G.E.'s technical service contracts across the world. I still didn't have a PC, so I cranked out reams of multi-columned, multicurrency, multicountry spreadsheets each month. And at the end of the year I was once again part of annual closing; this division sent even more reports to corporate headquarters. On the bright side, I finally had my own cubicle and a plastic nameplate.

In the time since I started with G.E., my salary had increased by fifty percent. But while I enjoyed the added security of a larger and larger salary, the money in itself wasn't as exciting as I thought it might be. I was happy that I could buy the things I needed, but never felt the desire to be extravagant— no fancy clothes or wild electronic equipment or elaborate holidays in the Caribbean. And while it was pleasant seeing larger numbers on my A.T.M. slips when I pressed "Balance," otherwise it meant little.

BUT DESPITE my newfound wealth, after two years in Manhattan, I had had enough with the high rents: it was time for a move. Rob had decided to buy a condo on the Upper East Side and, after a brief search, I found a place with a G.E. friend and his female roommate in Forest Hills, which meant a half-hour commute on the E train into Manhattan.

In December of 1985, I completed the Financial Management Program and, like all the trainees, I was elated to finish with the classes and the six-month rotations. We were fêted with a lavish graduation dinner on the top floor of an office building in Midtown, complete with guest speakers, awards, and diplomas. The program we had completed had proven difficult, and many hadn't made it through, so I was proud (and relieved) to have my certificate. And two weeks earlier, in lieu of a final rotation, I had accepted a "special project" assignment for one year; I was to help the company consolidate its accounts before closing down the office.

In the two years since I started, General Electric had already "downsized" thousands of employees. And a few months before I completed the training program, G.E. decided to lay off nearly all of the staff in my building in Manhattan. Since the primary work of the International Division was the accounting for the international business of other G.E. divisions, Corporate had decided to save money by shifting the finance work back onto the divisions. So, therefore, no need for the office in Manhattan. Besides, the building was itself valuable property which could be rented or sold.

While downsizing looked good on the balance sheet and undoubtedly helped to streamline the company, it meant letting go of employees who had worked with G.E. their entire adult lives. But traditionally, General Electric, like IBM and AT&T, was known for *not* laying people off and had, as a result, merited a tremendous amount of loyalty and personal sacrifice from their employees. G.E. counted on this loyalty and continually stressed the notion of the "G.E. family." The royal blue T-shirts handed out at company picnics said, "G.E. is ME!"

In April of 1984, the top managers had called the entire division staff into a large auditorium for a special presentation. Rumors of layoffs had been circulating for months but, as yet, we hadn't heard anything definite. One executive walked on stage in his shirtsleeves and stood behind a small podium. The lights dimmed and projected onto a large screen was a long column of numbers. We thought we were being shown some financial statistics. And, in a way, we were.

"As some of you may have heard," said the executive, "we are downsizing." There was audible stirring and shifting in seats.

"Here are how many people we have now," he said, pointing to a number: 400. "And here are how many we will have left at the end of the year." He pointed to another number: 50.

This, he explained, was part of G.E.'s strategy to make the company "lean and mean." G.E. would try to find jobs in other divisions across the country for as many people as they could, but since all of the divisions were cutting back, it was doubtful that many would be transferred. As it turned out, there were jobs available only for the younger, lower-level employees like myself and the other trainees. But for most of my friends in the auditorium, who had worked for decades with the company, there would be no possibility of employment.

"Any questions?"

The room fell silent. Most of the people in the room sat dumbfounded, with their heads down; a woman next to me dabbed her eyes delicately with a Kleenex.

The management stated that the company had no choice; it was simply a matter of economics. It was unfair, they said, to expect the company to retain people it didn't need. But strict economics was not the only reason that the employees had remained at G.E. for so long. Many longtime employees had offered great sacrifices for the company, fully expecting that when times got tough, the company would remember their loyalty and stand by them. Some of the older employees, for example, had moved their families to backwater locations for years at a time at the behest of the company. These people had come to expect at least some loyalty in return.

But the only employees spared were a few managers, the trainees, and a handful of people who would support the physical plant, that is, the maintenance staff of the building. Management gradually began to place the trainees in jobs vacated by the longtime employees.

That same month, during the downsizing, Jack Welch decided to renovate the CEO's office in the building. Though corporate headquarters were located in Connecticut, Welch enjoyed having a private office in New York, which he visited roughly two or three days a month. Since the building had in earlier years served as the corporate headquarters, there was still an enormous chairman's office on the forty-fifth floor, paneled in mahogany and boasting a sweeping view of Manhattan. After deciding the office was too stodgy for the 80s, Welch had it completely renovated, installing marble floors, teak walls, and a room-sized white oriental rug. So as downsized employees were carting out their boxes of personal

effects—their layoffs the result of cost-cutting measures—
workmen were bringing in the chairman's new teak walls and
wool carpets.

My assignment was to clean up the Plant and Equipment
ledger, which totaled roughly twenty million dollars. At the
time, it was "out of balance," much as someone's checkbook
might be, by an incredible two million dollars. It was, in short,
an accounting nightmare. The prevailing office wisdom was
that it would take most of the year to find the imbalances. The
person who previously held the job (an older, longtime
employee) was, not surprisingly, wholly uninterested in training the twenty-three-year-old who was taking over his job.
Hostile was a better word. He, therefore, did not provide me
with any information.

At Wharton, our Accounting 1A textbook had featured the
financial statements of fictional companies, hopelessly mis-
managed, with names like "Fly-by-Nite Enterprises" and "Mis-
managed Co." After working just a few days on the Plant and
Equipment account, it seemed as if the books of Fly-by-Nite
had miraculously sprung to life. The books were a depressing
mess and did not match the "subledger" account or details. In
other words, as a result of poor accounting records, the numbers on the company ledgers were grossly inaccurate and did
not at all represent the physical assets of the company. To deter-
mine what the correct balances should be, I began to track
down incorrect journal entries and invoices from ten and
twenty years prior. It began to get a little ridiculous. One day I
found myself rifling through a box of dog-eared journal entries
from 1958. I finally came up with a rule of thumb not to be held
responsible for any accounting entries made before I was born.

Fortunately, I worked with a good group of people in General Accounting. Most of us had been promised jobs in other
locations and were entrusted with the same task—that is, clean
up the books before the International Division was closed.
Together we shared an office on the eighth floor, with enormous windows that overlooked the corner of 51st Street and
Lexington Avenue. Though we were frazzled from the overtime

and stressed by the constant layoffs and departures of the employees who had trained us, we grew into a tight group. Certainly we saw more of one another than we did of our families, even on weekends.

As anyone who works in a large corporation discovers, this kind of office setting can become uniquely comfortable and comforting. Your coworkers are almost like a family whose foibles and eccentricities you come to know (but not always love). You participate in the smallest details of their lives by virtue of being with them for most of the day. The cast of office characters is diverse—the secretaries who know you better than some of your friends, the cafeteria workers who know what you eat and don't eat, the receptionists ready with sarcastic remarks when you're late for work, the coworkers with whom you spend eight hours a day, the naïve new recruits and the employees who have been with the company since before you were born.

But much of the time, sitting at my desk, surrounded by mountains of torn, faded invoices, yellowing bills, indecipherable journal entries, and ancient financial reports, I just wanted to throw in the towel. A few times a day a higher level manager—no doubt worried about losing his own job—visited us to bark out an order or berate us for not doing things more rapidly.

I ended up working most nights until 8:00, taking the subway home, grabbing some greasy Chinese food, and eating by myself in our apartment. My roommates also worked late, and I normally saw them only on weekends. Eventually, I began to work most weekends as well. Saturdays I took the train in from Queens, full of last night's drunks, early morning workers, and the odd beggar. Getting out at 53rd and Lex, I picked up a cup of coffee and a doughnut at a diner and settled in for another weekend of work at my desk. Bit by bit, others in the office trickled in, wearing jeans and sweatshirts, and plopped down in front of their desks with a groan. After a few months of this regimen, I began to notice a persistent stomachache. I chalked it up to the Chinese food and the late hours, and resolved to cut back on the shrimp lo mein. For the first time, I began to dislike my life.

My college friends asked me why I simply didn't quit. But failing to complete my assignment would have only translated into more work for the others in the office. Though my loyalty to G.E. might have diminished, I knew I couldn't let down my coworkers. After working a few hours on Saturdays, I would go for a break to the evening Mass at St. Patrick's Cathedral, a block away from the office. It was a quiet place to escape the stress of the job. I prayed and wondered how long this could go on. Even God, I thought, rested on the seventh day.

THAT FIRST SUMMER in Queens was miserable. We had a few small air conditioners in our apartment, which did little to improve the sticky New York summer air. And now that I had to take a daily ride on the subway, the heat became a real nuisance, as I stood on the stifling subway platform at 75th and Continental Avenue during the one-hundred-degree days with a suit and tie, sweating and praying that the train would be air-conditioned.

With all the subway trips back and forth from work, I discovered I had a tremendous amount of unused time. Reading the *New York Times* standing up with a hundred people pressing around me was something I had consistently failed to master, and it was almost impossible to wash the *Times'* ink from my fingers. So, instead, I decided to fill in some gaps in my education. Since I had placed out of the one English requirement at Wharton, the only literature course I had taken in college was the class in American poetry. I felt undereducated, at least in the liberal arts. So I read what I figured were things I should have read in college: *Portrait of the Artist as a Young Man, The Odyssey, The Iliad, The Aeneid, Anna Karenina, Madame Bovary.* When I finished *The Brothers Karamazov,* I told a friend who was a Russian studies major at Penn that I had skipped the part about the Grand Inquisitor and his interview with Jesus since it was so boring. "You're kidding!" he said. "It's probably the most important part of the book." But, at the time, Dostoevski's arcane theological questions were less interesting than the plot. In *The Iliad,* I read about spears being thrust through people's heads while the unsuspecting passengers on the E train calmly read their morning papers.

At one point during the summer I learned of a job at the Museum of Modern Art as a financial analyst. Even though it paid ten thousand dollars less than my current salary, I decided to interview. I was drawing closer to finishing my assignment, and I had my doubts about transferring to another G.E. division to take another dull finance job.

I walked into the museum, a few blocks away from my office, as I had many times before, but this time continued upstairs to the their finance department. The personnel man was surprised I was considering a salary cut. How could he be sure that I was serious about the job? "I'm here, aren't I?" I answered.

In a few days, they called to tell me I was overqualified. What was to stop me from leaving if I didn't like the job, especially if it was such a low salary? A good point, I had to admit. But for a little while I imagined myself working in the same building as the Cézannes, Picassos, and Monets. Telling people "I work at the Museum of Modern Art" would have sounded much better than "I look up invoices from 1965."

After a year of late nights, working weekends, and nausea, I finally finished the Plant and Equipment balances. I composed an exceedingly long report that detailed all the discoveries and the myriad corrections I had made over the past twelve months. Some of the errors had been squirreled away in fake accounts, but most of them were simply the result of incorrect accounting that I corrected in a one-time journal entry comprising of hundreds of lines.

I made an appointment with the head of our division, figuring I could play up the completion of the project. One morning in June, I proudly presented him with a one-page report and told him that, out of the two million dollars, I had located all but four thousand. I awaited the inevitable words of praise.

Instead, he glanced down my report—the project that had taken a full year of my days, nights, and weekends—looked up, and said, "Where's the rest of it?"

I could only blurt out, "Well, it's only four thousand dollars. I found almost all of the two million."

"You should have found it all," he said curtly, and went back to his work.

3.

An Unseen Hook

I wonder if you remember the story Mummy read to us the
evening Sebastian got drunk, the bad night. Father Brown
said something like, "I caught him (the thief) with an unseen
hook and an invisible line which is long enough to let him
wander to the ends of the world and still to bring him back
with a twitch upon the thread."

Evelyn Waugh, *Brideshead Revisited*

Luckily, I managed to land a position in the highly profitable
(and therefore extremely sexy) G.E. Credit Corporation,
which was expanding rapidly. G.E. Credit, based in Connecticut, was not only General Electric's financing arm but also an
enormous financial supermarket in its own right, with retail-
store financing, mortgage financing, transportation financing,
investment banking, and even a small commercial bank. G.E.
Credit, for example, served as the credit arm for companies like
Macy's and Apple Computers. When customers paid their
credit card bills to Macy's, they were actually mailing their
checks to G.E.-run processing centers throughout the country.
The money was from G.E., the processing of payments was
completed by G.E. All Macy's did was pay us a fee.

G.E. Credit, also known as GECC, had also saved General
Electric Company millions of dollars in taxes by purchasing
dozens of airplanes and renting them back to the airlines. This
was known as a "sale-leaseback" and, in this way, we were able
to earn government tax credits for purchasing "investment
equipment," though we never used the planes ourselves. This

was just one of their many profitable financing deals. Were
G.E. Credit a bank, the company was fond of pointing out, it
would be the seventh largest in the nation.

I took a job managing G.E. Credit's Financial Management
Program, the same training program I had recently completed
in New York, mainly because I thought it would be more interesting than another thankless accounting job. I had had enough
of looking up thirty-year-old invoices. Taking a job in human
resources would probably torpedo my chances of another
finance job, but I wasn't overly concerned. Maybe the new job
would allow me to be more creative.

The "downside," as they said at G.E., was moving to Stamford, Connecticut. From the City that Never Sleeps to one that
apparently never did anything but. Stamford was fine if you
were a member of the Connecticut landed gentry, but for a yuppie it was pretty boring. Stamford proper in the mid-80s was
undergoing a building boom—sleek corporate office towers
were popping up downtown and sylvan office "campuses"
sprouted further out in the country. But the boom ended there.
When I arrived in 1985, there were three decent restaurants and
two movie theaters in the whole town.

But so what? There were worse places to live. The job certainly sounded more interesting than the one I had just left. And
the money was great. I took an apartment in Stamford with two
other longtime G.E. people, neither of whom I knew. But at this
point, so many of my friends had been transferred from New
York to Stamford that I felt at home immediately.

In the new position, I hired people right out of college and,
as was the practice in New York, placed them in various "rotations" in different GECC departments. Since G.E. Credit was so
profitable, we had dozens of branches and, therefore, all sorts of
great rotations for the trainees. The better a trainee did on his (or
her) performance evaluations and in the courses, the more
chance he (or she) had of winning one of the more desirable
assignments—which included positions in London, Frankfurt,
San Francisco, Chicago, and Raleigh. There were also other
perks: in London and Frankfurt, for example, the company paid

for the trainees' rent. Generous Electric. And since the U.S. dollar was strong and the working environment overseas a good deal more relaxed, an international rotation meant a six-month break in a fully furnished apartment in Europe. They were popular assignments.

My first manager at GECC was a delightful woman in her mid-thirties named Alice. She was highly respected in the company, had herself completed the financial training program, and was fun to work with to boot. Alice was very much of a "high pot" at G.E.—as in "high potential." There were high pots and low pots. No one wanted to be a low pot.

And I finally had my own office. The office had a door (my first) and floor-to-ceiling windows, which gave me a view of a stupendously ugly bronze fountain that stood outside on the lawn. Also, as everyone noted, my office had twelve lights in the ceiling instead of the usual eight. (This was considered quite an accomplishment.)

I found I enjoyed running the training program in Stamford, since I had more contact with people than in my previous jobs. For one thing, the job included lots of interviewing, since I was responsible for filling the trainee positions with recent college grads.

Interviewing was fun—and "fun" was certainly a new sensation at work. Among other things, I organized the coveted "second interviews" for college seniors who were invited to visit our offices after the initial on-campus interview. In addition to meeting with me, I arranged for recruits to meet with two trainees and a few upper-level managers. After everyone completed an evaluation on the candidate, Alice and I sat down and decided whom to hire. My favorite part of the job was calling up the students to offer them a job. It was still close enough to my own college experience that I remembered how wonderful it felt to be on the other end.

The interviews took up a good deal of time, but I didn't much mind. And few interviews lacked surprises. One young woman lost her luggage at the airport in New York, and so was forced to arrive at our office sporting the same clothes she'd been wearing on the plane, which unfortunately included a bright pink sweatshirt that said, "I'm with Stupid." She wore this during all of her interviews, and it turned out to be something of an icebreaker. We eventually hired her.

Another young man, during the course of a lunchtime interview, stopped me in the middle of my explanation of how wonderful the training program was, and asked, if I wasn't going to finish my peas, could he please have them? Of course, the recruits were nervous and ended up doing things that they probably wouldn't normally do. One recruit, gamely struggling to eat his pasta while he explained why he wanted to work for me, twirled his spaghetti rapidly around his fork and neatly sprayed tomato sauce clear across the table and onto my tie. For a brief moment I thought he was going to faint. We hired him anyway.

And another asked, in all seriousness, since he had to buy a car to get to work, would we reimburse him for the one he had just bought?

Deciding on whom to hire was easier than I had expected. Most of the people distinguished themselves within a few minutes as definite hires or definite passes. And rather than using run-of-the-mill interview questions (What are your strengths? What kind of tree would you be if you were a tree?)—which only elicited canned answers (I work hard. I'd be a strong but flexible tree.)—I found I could unearth what I needed to know with a well-timed "Oh really?"

During the course of one interview, for example, an accomplished young man from a good school announced, out of the blue, that one of the reasons he was interested in working for G.E. was that he preferred working with "intelligent people."

I wasn't sure what he meant. Did he mean, I asked, that he'd worked with intelligent types before and that it had been a good experience?

"Well, not really," he answered. "It's more that I don't like being around stupid people."

"Oh really?" I said.

"Yeah. You know how you walk around in malls and you see people shopping at discount stores for their clothes? And you think, these losers probably couldn't even get a real job. Their lives are so . . . *pathetic*."

This revealing gem was something you wouldn't get from a standard interview question. He received the unusually-high-number-of-applicants-this-year-makes-it-difficult-to-extend-offers-to-everyone letter.

The job was also my first position of any real authority, as it included responsibilities for hiring and placement. And while at first I tried to assume an air of *gravitas*, I nevertheless ended up becoming friends with the trainees, who were, after all, only two years younger than I. It didn't hurt the working relationships; if anything it seem to make the trainees more open with me. And I decided early on to be truthful with them about working at G.E., rather than simply feeding them the company line. Alice's manager, for example, wanted us to push the less desirable jobs, but I didn't think that was fair. It was obvious that the trainees were clever enough to recognize when they were being misled. Instead, I was blunt about the good rotations and the bad rotations. This made me less of a star with management, but kept me on a more even footing with the trainees.

I also tried hard to dream up new programs and events that would make the company more interesting for the trainees. A few months into the job, I took the trainees to G.E. Corporate Headquarters in Fairfield, a few minutes up the road from Stamford.

G.E.'s corporate headquarters were designed to evoke awe. Two large, white, three-story buildings are set into a hill overlooking acres of the peaceful Connecticut countryside. G.E. had, in fact, purchased the acreage that comprised their sylvan "view" across I-95 to ensure that it remained just that—an uncluttered, undeveloped view for the visual pleasure of G.E.'s top executives. And given the lack of what G.E. considered a suitably posh hotel in the area (unless you counted the Hi-Ho Motel on I-95), G.E. built their own. The regal "Guest House," as it was called, served as the temporary home to visiting G.E. executives. Like Jack Welch's office in New York, it had teak walls and plush white carpets.

The visit to Corporate was designed to give the trainees a glimpse of the fantastic job opportunities that awaited them after they completed their training. A few weeks before, I had met with the head of Corporate Dining Services to plan the food that we would serve during the day. He also ran the CEO's private dining room and prepared the food served on G.E.'s corporate jets. His job, he boasted, was to provide the chairman and his guests with any type of food at any time.

In addition to the food, the highlight of the day was a talk from one of the top finance executives in the entire G.E. empire: a short, dour man who I'll call Dan. (The names used in the forthcoming corporate horror stories have been changed, out of charity.) After a tedious speech on how interesting finance was, Dan asked for questions.

"I have one," said a woman who had now worked at G.E. Credit for a few months. "You know," she said, rising from her seat, "G.E. expects us to work a lot of overtime and sacrifice a lot of our personal life."

"That's right," Dan answered coolly.

"And I guess my question is whether . . . "

"I *know* what your question is," he shouted before she could finish. "Your question is what does G.E. owe *me*. Well, get this straight: G.E. doesn't owe you a damn *thing!*"

Now, it was bad enough to *suspect* that the upper-ups thought that way, but it was quite another to hear them admit it in a public forum. Corporate loyalty was apparently a one-sided proposition. It was, I think, at that moment that I lost whatever allegiance to G.E. that still remained.

To an even greater extent than in New York, "lean and mean" here was meant quite literally, with an emphasis on mean. Some executives seemed to lack any conception of human dignity and would regularly and gleefully humiliate their subordinates. No matter how human the company tried to be ("G.E. is ME!"), the income statement remained the top priority. Of course this was to be expected. We were in the business of making money for stockholders, as are all companies. But efforts to persuade us of the company's vaunted care and concern for its employees in the face of what I witnessed daily struck me as more than a little ironic.

A few months into my job, Alice left to have a child. I was sorry to see her go. I ended up working for a succession of managers, one of whom I'll call Karen. This manager was a high pot, too, but much more corporate than Alice, and less relaxed.

One of the first recruits Karen and I discussed was a black woman from a small Southern college. She was energetic and bright but also very overweight. I wanted to hire her. My manager, however, thought otherwise.

"She just doesn't portray the right image, Jim," said my manager. "And you know that as well as I do."

Well, I knew what she meant, so I pushed her on it.

"You mean because she's black?" I asked.

"Of *course* not."

"Because she's fat?"

"No," Karen said, "and stop putting words in my mouth. You *know* what I mean."

"What is it, exactly?"

"Oh, please," she snapped. "What would the CEO think if he saw someone who looks like *her* walking down the hall?"

I remember thinking, well, I hope he would think to look beyond just her appearance. But I was too surprised to say *anything*, having just heard a narrow-minded explanation of the right "image" from, of all people, a human resource executive. And we were the ones who were supposed to know better! Conversations like this made me wonder if I was in the right place.

Fortunately, I enjoyed my peers at G.E. Credit who, almost to a person, were intelligent and compassionate. It was great being around so many friends around my age. The problem was what I used to call the Jackass Theory. That is, the higher some executives rose in the company, the more of a jackass they seemed to become. To survive in G.E., you had to be tough, almost impervious to criticism, willing to dump on others, work your butt off, and be able to triumph in Machiavellian maneuverings. Eventually—with some notable exceptions—

you could become a Total Jackass, insulated from any criticism, short-tempered with your subordinates, and completely wedded to your job.

One of the top finance guys in our division, Karen's boss, was a craggy-faced older man named Len, who had been with the company for about a thousand years. Though he was only two levels above my manager, he was a quasi-mythical figure who almost never appeared at our office, only one floor below his. I had visited Len's enormous office only once, when my manager was out sick, and was privileged to spend about three minutes in his sullen, glassy-eyed presence.

At one point, Len decided that to reward the top performers in our division, he would host a monthly luncheon. Each month, Karen selected five lucky employees who, as a result of their performance, were to be plucked from corporate obscurity and join Len in the executive dining room for an hour-long lunch. In this way, Len would get to know the employees and vice versa.

One day, around noon, I was sitting in my office working on my PC and heard the secretaries grow ominously quiet outside my door. Into my office walked Len, down from Mount Olympus.

"Len," I said stupidly, as I rose from my chair.

"Where's my lunch?" he barked. His rheumy eyes glistened.

"Excuse me?"

"Where's my damn *lunch*? There's no one in the damn dining room. I've been waiting ten minutes!"

I knew instantly what had happened. Somehow the invitations had gotten screwed up. Fortunately, I had nothing to do with it.

"Um, well, Karen handles that, I think and I . . . "

"*Get her,*" he said through clenched teeth. (I remember thinking that I had never seen anyone actually clench his teeth.)

Karen was in the middle of an interview. I walked out of my office, with Len trailing me. I knocked on Karen's door; I knew she detested being interrupted.

"What *is* it?" she shouted through the closed door.

Before I could answer, Len reached around me and opened the door.

"Len!" said Karen. She leapt from her chair.

"Where's my *lunch?*"

For a moment I thought that Karen would go to the cafeteria and fix him a sandwich. But before she could answer, he provided a helpful explanation.

"There's *no one* in the dining room. I've been waiting around for fifteen minutes!" (I noted that he had revised his waiting time.)

Karen said that there must have been a problem with the invitations. She asked her secretary, but neither of them could figure out what had happened. Obviously, though, no one had received the invitations. In the middle of her explanation, Len walked out in a red-faced huff. Poor Karen, I thought. She worked hard and certainly didn't deserve this. (I also thought: I'm glad it wasn't me.)

It was ridiculous. I wondered why Len couldn't have found at least *some* humor in the situation. He could just have easily told us of the mix-up and—gasp!—even laughed about it. Instead, his first reaction was to scream at someone and assign blame.

Later, I was handed the responsibility for Len's lunches. I sent out the invitations to everyone one month in advance and was instructed to call the employees the day before as a reminder and then, finally, the morning of the lunch.

After working with people like Len, I began to find it impossible to aspire to such positions. I couldn't envision myself behaving the way that Len and many of the higher-level managers did. So I socialized with people at my own level. Karen told me one day that she didn't approve of this.

"Why not?" I asked.

"Optics, Jim."

"Optics?"

"Yes," she said. "I want you to spend more time around senior-level managers. You're always having lunch with your peers and the trainees. It doesn't look good. And the managers notice this, I have to tell you."

At this point, I began to feel trapped. *What* was I doing in this environment? For that matter, how ever did I *get* here? I couldn't imagine myself (or rather it was too *frightening* to imagine myself) ending up a Jackass. Maybe I was one already.

Many of the people with whom I worked were also discouraged about work. Since I spent a good part of my job listening to people talk about their jobs, I knew that only a few found their work enjoyable. Many of my coworkers focused instead on what the jobs could lead to. The job, therefore, was just a means to an end. And many of the trainees were anxious to move immediately into graduate business schools after finishing the training program. While the company was obviously training the recruits for long careers at G.E., the trainees quickly recognized the cachet of the G.E. name in business schools, and many wanted out. As a result, I wrote a lot of B-school recommendations.

One of the trainees at the time, named Bill, asked me to review his own application to the Harvard Business School. The main essay question, as it turned out, was to describe an "ethical dilemma" that the applicant had faced. Bill described a manager's asking him to falsify financial results that would effect someone's compensation. In other words, his essay said that he had been asked to lie on a financial report to help someone get a better bonus. This was more than a little disturbing, since Bill technically worked for me and I had never heard about this incident.

"When did *this* happen?" I asked him, astonished.

"Well, it really didn't happen exactly like that," he admitted. "I couldn't come up with an ethical dilemma so I had to make one up."

"Let me get this straight," I said. "You're *lying* on an ethical dilemma question?"

He failed to see the irony. I suggested, instead, that he use this very situation as his ethical dilemma—that he was tempted to cheat on his application to get into Harvard. That, I pointed out, was a real ethical dilemma. Instead, Bill opted for the first, false one. He started at Harvard the next fall.

G.E. THAT YEAR went through an "image change." Management lamented that when most American consumers thought of G.E., they still thought of lightbulbs, when, in fact, this was just a miniscule part of G.E. With divisions like Medical Systems, Aerospace, Plastics. and G.E. Credit, General Electric was anxious to communicate a new company image. So we officially became GE, instead of General Electric. And G.E. Credit (which sounded like we financed refrigerators) became GE Capital. The hallowed G.E. logo, or "meatball," was even changed, though so slightly that most of us couldn't see the difference. (The curlicues were downsized.) The company also changed their letterhead type to slanted letters in order to, as the memo said, "accentuate the positive dynamism of the company." We were also instructed not to refer to General Electric as General Electric in correspondence or over the phone. Just GE. And not G.E. Just GE. Periods were out. Apparently, periods were not dynamic enough.

I, too, went through something of an "image change" in 1986. I was promoted to "Specialist—Corporate Financial Management Development" which, besides giving me the longest title in the company, meant that I hired and placed people in mid-level finance jobs throughout the G.E. Credit Corporation, or rather, GE Capital. I would still have contact with the trainees, since I was staying in the same department, and would also help to "place" some of the graduates that I had worked with. With the promotion also came a great deal more work and far more overtime. Not only did I have to see everyone in the company looking for a new finance job, but every manager looking to replace someone in his department came knocking on my door. Plus I was responsible for salary calculations and any "counseling" that needed to be done. This made me a popular person in the company, since I now had all the dope on the newest openings and knew pretty much everything that was going on in the company.

In my new position, I also discovered that employees were classified by personnel groupings—beyond just hi pot or low pot. After your yearly performance appraisals, you were assigned a number which summarized your potential. A "one" meant that you were promotable by two salary levels, a "two" meant one salary level. "Threes" were not promotable at all, and a "four" meant you were on your way out. It very much reminded me of *Brave New World*—you were your number. Managers called up asking for a job candidate and, after I provided a lengthy explanation of someone's strengths or weaknesses, they would say, "Yeah, that's fine, but is she a one?" Or, "Forget it, she's just a two." Or, "Jim, do you have any ones for me?" Like we were playing Fish. With people.

Around the same time as the new job, my parents decided to separate for a while, and I began fielding almost nightly calls from my mother. This, along with the extra work from the new job, made me feel miserable and, not surprisingly, stressed out. Within a few months, what I thought were some minor stomachaches from too much greasy Chinese food developed into what the doctors called "irritable bowel syndrome," a stress-related illness. After eating almost anything, I experienced stabbing pains in my stomach. No problem, said the doctor at GE, just avoid the following: greasy foods, fried foods, spicy foods, milk products. It became a challenge for my friends to find a restaurant we could go to: no Mexican, no Chinese, no Indian. But the most important thing, the doctor said, was to avoid any stress. I found it more than a little amusing that a fellow GE employee could say this with a straight face.

As an official "human resource" person, I was now privileged to see what went on behind the proverbial closed doors. A few months into the new job, one of the company's mid-level managers visited my office and announced, "My boss has decided to fire Mike."

I was shocked. Mike had been with GE for fifteen years and had, just the year before, received a company incentive award for his performance: an all-expense paid trip to a plush resort hotel in Arizona. I thought it was bizarre that he would now be fired.

I approached the manager, named Bill, and asked him what was going on. Since assuming his managerial position six weeks earlier, Bill said, he had decided that he did not want Mike on his staff any longer.

"I wanna bounce him," Bill said, using a favorite company expression.

"But you can't," I said, "we just gave him an incentive award and no one's documented any poor performance. In fact, you haven't even mentioned you were dissatisfied!"

"So *what?*" said Bill, leaning back in his swivel chair. "I've already fired him."

"But he's been with the company for fifteen years and it's going to be practically impossible for him to get a job. I mean, have some compassion."

His answer was short and memorable.

"Fuck compassion," he said.

My only recourse was to go over his head and see Bill's boss, the manager of our division. I repeated the conversation word for word and, in case he didn't get the point, reminded him that because of Mike's age and the complete lack of any poor performance records, the company would probably get slapped with an age-discrimination suit. He picked up his phone and barked to his secretary, "Get Bill in here now!"

When Bill arrived, his boss confronted him with the situation that I had just laid out. Bill looked over at me and said blandly, "Oh, Jim must have misunderstood. I never meant I'd fire Mike. He's far too valuable."

"You'd better not," screamed the manager. "If you don't like him, you damn well better find a new place for him!" At least he believed me. But the whole thing disgusted me.

ALL OF THIS prompted me to give renewed and more serious thought to looking for something new, to doing "something else." At this point, I realized that I had achieved most of the goals that I dreamed about in college: I was making a great salary, had a good deal of independence and control at work, and was moving up in the company. But those things in themselves didn't bring me much satisfaction. Simply put, I couldn't figure out the *point* of what I was doing with my life. Something basic was missing. I enjoyed my coworkers and some of the work in human resources, but what was the point of the work itself? Is this life?

I attempted to envision my job in terms of whom I was helping. Well, I was certainly helping the people who came to me for counseling or who were in tough situations on the job. But if that was the point, then why not work with people in need all of the time, instead of just some of the time? And if the money has no great appeal, why not do something more, well, charitable?

At Mass that Sunday, the reading from the Gospel of Luke was of the rich young man who approaches Jesus. The man asks Jesus what he must to do enter the Kingdom of God. "You know the commandments," says Jesus. "I have kept all these since my youth," answers the man. "There is still one more thing lacking," Jesus says. "Sell all that you own and distribute the money to the poor, and you will have treasure in heaven. Then come, follow me." But the young man goes away sad, since he is very rich.

That was me—a rich, young (and depressed) man. So I started to consider other things to do with my life. Tentatively, at first.

Until this point, I had been a good, if unremarkable, Catholic. I still went to Mass every Sunday at a nearby parish church, called St. Leo the Great. The church was a few miles down the road from the office, which made it easier to frequent when I worked Saturdays or Sundays. And it was one of the few modern churches that I found beautiful. A simple, airy design, with an altar sunlit from above by a wide skylight. The homilies were compelling, thanks to an intelligent group of priests who never talked down to the congregation. Sunday Mass at St. Leo's was an oasis of clarity in the midst of a desert of confusion and indecision.

In the midst of this indecision, I came home one night from work at 8:00. I had had a wretched day—spending two hours with an employee who hated her job so much that her hands shook noticeably. I tried to convince her to see our in-house psychologist, but she was too embarrassed. She thought she might have to quit. I myself wasn't feeling particularly well either. I dreaded the next day when I would have to confront her difficult and mean-spirited manager, who thought she was malingering. It also looked like I would probably have to work during the weekend. I was dead tired, too tired to think about making dinner, so I turned on the TV.

There was a special on PBS called "Merton: A Film Biography," about a man named Thomas Merton. All sorts of well-known people appeared on the screen and praised him as a powerful and lasting influence in their lives. Whoever Thomas Merton was, he had evidently made a vivid impression on these people. After a few minutes, I realized that they were talking about a Trappist monk who had lived (or was living, I wasn't sure) somewhere in the hills of Kentucky. His autobiography was called *The Seven Storey Mountain* and, when it published in 1948, it was a surprise best-seller. To my dismay, I had heard of neither him nor his book. I only caught the last part of the show, but it was sufficiently interesting that the next day I began to search for the book. Tracking it down in Stamford was difficult, but I finally found one copy.

The Seven Storey Mountain is a beautiful story. Thomas Merton was born in France, the son of a woman who died young, leaving Tom to live with his father, a peripatetic painter. After spending most of his childhood in France, Tom was sent to England to Oakham, a secondary school he detested. After his father died, Tom entered Cambridge University, where he led a rather dissolute student life and (though this is omitted in his autobiography) fathered a child. As a result of this disgrace, Tom was sent to the States in the 1930s to live with his mother's family in Long Island, and then to continue his schooling at Columbia University.

As a young man, Thomas Merton felt perpetually ill at ease with almost everything—including himself. But gradually, and mysteriously, he decides to become a Catholic. He is baptized and, to the surprise of his friends, quickly declares his intention to enter the Franciscan Order. After an attack of scruples, he tells the Franciscans about his sordid past—including the illegitimate child. Not surprisingly for 1940, the Franciscans wouldn't have him. After confessing his sins to a friar in New York City, he is told bluntly that he is completely unfit to become a priest. Tom is disconsolate and, casting about for something to do, he makes a retreat at a Trappist monastery in Kentucky, called Our Lady of Gethsemani.

He arrives at the monastery late in the night. "Have you come to stay?" asks the brother at the door. Merton recounts his reaction:

> The question terrified me. It sounded too much like the voice of my own conscience.
> "Oh no!" I said. "Oh no." And I heard my whisper echoing around the hall and vanishing up the indefinite, mysterious heights of a dark and empty stair-well above our heads. The place smelled frighteningly clean, old and clean, an ancient house, polished and swept and repainted and repainted over and over, year after year.
> "What's the matter? Why can't you stay? Are you married or something?" said the Brother.
> "No," I said lamely. "I have a job . . . "

But after battling with himself for a few months, Merton decides that he does, in fact, want to be a monk. He enters the monastery in 1941.

Wow. I realized with some force that this was what I could do. Maybe not join a monastery, but at least move closer to a life like that. It sounded great—so peaceful, so romantic. I couldn't get his story out of my mind, and read the book three times.

The Seven Storey Mountain was written a few years after Merton had entered the monastery in Kentucky, in the "first fervor" of his religious vocation. Only a few years later, he would label his early writings as overly pious and excessively critical of "the world." Nevertheless, the religious life he described exerted a strong romantic pull, speaking to a deep longing inside of me. Thomas Merton seemed to have struggled with the same problems I did: vanity, false ambition, careerism. The more he confessed his shortcomings, the more I felt the urge to listen to what he had to say, and the more resonance I felt within me.

I tried to find other books by Thomas Merton. At this point I had no idea if he was "famous" or not. I mentioned him to a few of my friends, but no one had heard of him. Maybe he was some sort of discredited "cult" figure in the Church. I wasn't sure. Thinking there might be a sequel to *The Seven Storey Mountain* (the story ends shortly after he enters the monastery), I began searching for it. Instead, I found a book of his meditations entitled *No Man Is an Island*, and idly flipping through it came upon this passage:

> Why do we try to spend our lives striving to be something that we would never want to be, if we only knew what we wanted? Why do we waste our time doing things which, if we only stopped to think about them, are just the opposite of what we were made for?

That was me! It was so clear. I didn't feel as if I were at all *made* for the life I was leading. And though I didn't know *what* I was made for, Thomas Merton's way seemed closer to me than the corporate way.

I began reading other "religious" books as well: C. S. Lewis's *Surprised by Joy*, an Oxford don's account of his conversion; George Bernanos's *Diary of a Country Priest*, the story of a simple, holy parish priest in rural France. Reading was about the only way I could explore what was going on inside of me and not give myself away. For I was profoundly embarrassed by the idea of thinking about religion so much, and even *considering* acting on these thoughts. It was attractive but, at the same time, weird.

Still, I couldn't get it out of my mind that I wanted to be a priest or a monk or a brother or . . . something. Anything that would bring me closer to the feelings I had. In the end, of course, this was what some people refer to as a "call"—the happy inability to think of anything else. But I wouldn't realize this until later. At the time, it was just a minor obsession.

There were also some problems that seemed insurmountable. For one thing, I had little idea of what priests actually did outside of celebrating Mass. What exactly was a Franciscan? A Benedictine? A Jesuit? In the parish bulletins at St. Leo's, I noticed that some of the priests had letters after their names: O.S.B., O.F.M., S.J. Were these academic degrees? Did they represent the types of schools they went to? I wasn't sure.

I had certainly never spent any time with priests, unless you count confessions and the annual visits to our house by the parish priests. On the other hand, not having attended a Catholic school meant that I wasn't saddled with any stereotypes: the disciplinarian priest; the cold, ascetic priest; or even the chummy "Going My Way" Bing Crosby-type priest. I didn't know *any* priests, so I had no preconceptions.

In any event, I found it nearly impossible to put the idea out of my mind. Some days I would convince myself of the foolishness of even *thinking* in those terms. After all, I had worked hard to get into Wharton, and spent years studying business and climbing up the corporate ladder. Leaving would be a waste. All of those years down the drain. Plus, I was clearly running away from things that were too painful in my life—my family problems, the job stress, the stomach stuff. So why was it still so attractive?

I had no idea with whom to speak. Was there an office in the diocese that dealt with this? Or did I have to call some national office? Eventually, I cornered my parish priest at St. Leo's after

Mass one Sunday and finally blurted out, "I think I'd like to be a priest."

The words made me cringe. I hoped he wouldn't laugh. "You should probably contact the local vocations office," he said, not laughing. "And you might as well talk to the Jesuits up at Fairfield."

The vocations office in the diocese sounded like a good idea. But I had no idea who the Jesuits were or what they did. I was dimly aware that some Catholic colleges were run by the Jesuits: Fordham, Georgetown, Boston College (maybe Notre Dame—was that Jesuit?). I had heard of their founder, St. Ignatius of Loyola, and wondered why there were so many colleges named Loyola. Were they the same college with different campuses?

Wandering around the bookstores in Stamford, I continued my search for the sequel to Thomas Merton's story, hoping that I could find out what happened to him. Did he remain a Trappist? Did he leave the monastery? Was he happy? There was a list of books on the inside cover of his autobiography, maybe one of them would be the sequel. Instead, I stumbled upon a book called *The Jesuits: The Society of Jesus and the Betrayal of the Roman Catholic Church*. It was written by a disgruntled ex-Jesuit and seemed to be surprisingly negative, but at least it told me a few things about the group.

From this book it emerged that the Jesuits (whose formal name was the Society of Jesus) are a religious order and, as such, live lives of poverty, chastity, and obedience in community with one another. There are ordained Jesuits (priests) and nonordained Jesuits (brothers) who, since they are not attached to any diocese, are free to work anywhere. A diocesan priest, trained in a local seminary, is usually attached to one particular diocese for his career as a parish priest or administrator. The Jesuits, run by a general superior in Rome, were free to be missioned anywhere. They seemed free to do almost any type of work.

I liked that immediately. Unlike a monk, a Jesuit could work outside of the religious community. "Contemplatives in action" was the phrase that kept popping up. Jesuits are best known as teachers—but there are also Jesuit doctors, lawyers, architects, artists, actors, parish priests, prison chaplains, social workers, and authors. And I found out, to my initial dismay, that they are the Church's largest missionary order. (I definitely couldn't see myself doing *that*.) They count among their members St. Francis Xavier, one of the most famous Catholic missionaries. And, at least according to this particularly critical book, they were *very* controversial and had recently run into trouble with Pope John Paul II.

Since the Jesuits instantly appealed to me more than the diocesan priesthood, I decided to start with them. And now that I had read all the books about priests one could purchase in southern Connecticut, I figured I had gone as far as I could go without telling anyone of my desires. So, as embarrassed as I was, I contacted the Jesuits at Fairfield University for some information.

I closed the door to my office one day, called Fairfield, and asked to talk to one of the Jesuits.

"Jesuit Community!" someone answered brightly.

"Um, yeah, do you think I could get some information about . . . uh . . . joining the Jesuits?" Again, I grimaced when I heard my words. The priest on the phone suggested I come by the next day to pick up some information. I hung up the phone and quietly opened my office door. Apparently no one had overheard me.

The next day at lunch, I drove the few miles to Fairfield University, a small campus with wide green lawns and fresh-scrubbed, young, white, and (apparently) Catholic students. The Jesuit Community looked like a cross between a large classroom building and a hotel. Beside the main entrance was a white statue of a saint holding a book. An older man greeted me at the door. I told him I was there for some information about the Jesuits.

"So are you interested in becoming a Jesuit?"

"Uh, well, I have a job now. So, I'm sort of just . . . um . . . checking things out."

"Well, here's some information for you," he said, holding out a few brochures. "Would you like to talk a little bit about it?" "Well, I'm really busy!" I said emphatically. "I have to go! I work in Stamford. Thanks anyway."

He handed me the pamphlets. I said thanks again and returned to my car to flip through the brochures. Some of the information was useful, including a short book called *The Fifth Week*, written by a Jesuit about the vows of poverty, chastity, and obedience, life in community, and the "formation," or training period, that lasted—I found this hard to believe—ten years. Ten years! I could be a brain surgeon in less time.

One of the pamphlets helped to explain the "formation" program, which is similar to the one originally laid out by St. Ignatius Loyola. The first two years are spent in a novitiate, where a Jesuit novice learns about Jesuit spirituality and community life and also spends time in various Jesuit works. Typically, he also works with the poor, often in a developing country. Novices also make a thirty-day retreat based on the plan laid out in St. Ignatius Loyola's *Spiritual Exercises,* whatever that was. Thirty days, in silence. That seemed a bit excessive.

After two years, assuming he is happy as a Jesuit, a novice pronounces vows of poverty, chastity, and obedience. Then follows two years of philosophy studies in one of the Jesuit universities in the U.S. After philosophy, one works two years during a period known as "regency." Many Jesuits, said the pamphlets, teach in high schools during regency, some work overseas, others work in fields related to their experience before they enter the order. An architect, for example, might spend his regency building low-income housing in the developing world. After regency, for those who are planning to be ordained, comes four years of theology, then ordination. Finally, at the end of formation, comes a period called "tertianship," so called because it's seen as the "third year" of novitiate formation, where a Jesuit does yet another thirty-day retreat.

When I finished my quick reading of the book and the pamphlets I decided, "Well, I'm certainly not going to do *that*." It was too absurd. I liked the part about working with the poor and living in community and becoming a priest, but the part about the thirty-day retreat, the work overseas, and the stuff about "vows" seemed bizarre. Vows might be okay for Thomas Merton in the 1940s, but not for someone like me today.

By this time, I was *very* embarrassed that I had gone to Fairfield. Thank God I hadn't really made any sort of commitments to talk with anyone about it! I hoped that no one had seen me there.

So I tried putting it all out of my mind for the next two years. But I kept getting cheery letters from the Jesuits of New England telling me when their next "candidates' meeting" would be. That's what they called people who had expressed an interest in them—"candidates." For the next two years, cream-colored envelopes would show up with alarming regularity in my mailbox announcing an event or talk or meeting or Mass, invariably near Boston. I started off politely returning the cards and checking the box marked: "No. I will not be able to make it."

Eventually, I began tearing up the letters *at* the mailbox, fearing that my roommates might see them and ask me about them. And so I tried my best to forget about the Jesuits.

Part II

Come and See

*When Jesus turned and saw them following, he said
to them, "What are you looking for?" They said to
him, "Rabbi, where are you staying?" He said to
them, "Come and see."*

John 1:38–39

4.

A Bruised Reed

He will not cry or lift up his voice,
or make it heard in the street;
a bruised reed he will not break,
and a smoldering wick he will not quench;
he will faithfully bring forth justice.

Isaiah 42:2–3

With all the stress from work, the stress from home, and the stress from being sick all the time, I grew ever more miserable. Everything was starting to get to me, and I could feel myself inexorably becoming a different person—more easily depressed, more cranky, more cynical.

I complained to my friends, all of whom offered a variation of the following suggestions: first, quit your job. This was certainly tempting, but unrealistic. Second, just ignore your parents' problems. This, while healthy, I found almost impossible to do. I loved them too much. Finally, take a long vacation. Also healthy, but not much help in the long term.

One of my roommates remarked, "Why don't you see the E.A.P. person?" The Employee Assistance Program representative was an in-house psychologist who did excellent work with the many stressed-out employees at GE. I regularly referred employees—like the woman with the shaking hands—to her as part of my job. But, I told my roommate, I certainly was not in need of a psychologist.

"Oh, go ahead!" said my roommate. "What's the big deal? You send enough people to her yourself."

The next day I got my first-ever migraine headache, which temporarily clouded my vision and prevented me from reading. It was disconcerting, to say the least. I told my secretary what was happening and ducked out of the office, staggered down the hall, and stopped in to see the nurse. After she reassured me that I was fine, I returned to my office, though still unable to see clearly.

"Are you going blind?" asked my secretary dryly when I returned. "I could write my phone messages bigger." This was all the convincing I needed to see the E.A.P. woman.

The following morning I visited her office and poured out all of my problems. Though she was very competent, it didn't take a psychological genius to see that most of my physical problems were stress related. After listening for an hour, she suggested I see a "biofeedback specialist." I rolled my eyes.

"She's *very* good," she replied. "And you should probably see her partner, too."

Why not? Generous Electric was paying for it.

The biofeedback lady, named Anne, had an office in Westport, one of the tonier towns in Fairfield County. Her quiet office smelled of potpourri and was filled with baskets of dried flowers and *Country Life* magazines. On my first visit she asked me to sit in a leather easy chair as she hooked my fingers to sensors attached to a computer. I wondered if this was the same as a polygraph test. I told her how doubtful I was about all of this. "How can you possibly control your body?" I asked.

Anne smiled serenely. "Just relax and concentrate on the computer screen." While the first part might be a problem, I said, staring at a computer screen was a skill I had mastered over the last six years.

The screen showed five colored bars that went up and down and beeped musically. High beeps as the bars went up on the screen, and lower tones when they grew shorter.

"Okay," she said, "See if you can get the beeps to go lower."

It sounded stupid, but I tried anyway. Suprisingly, in a few minutes I had succeeded. "Now," she explained pointing to the colored bars on the screen, "this measure is your heart rate, this is your body temperature, and this measures electrical pulses on your skin. See, you've already got your body temp down by ten degrees."

Instant conversion. It really worked; all I had to do was to pay attention to the beeping. After an hour we talked about setting up weekly appointments. Anne also gave me a cassette tape which I was instructed to play on my Walkman at home. I popped it into my car tape deck: "Every day in every way, I'm getting better and better," said the dulcet voice on the tape. Boy, I *really* must be going off the deep end if she was giving me something like that. But I used it anyway.

The next session I was able to get the little bars on the screen to go even lower. Anne began asking me questions while I was hooked up.

"Now," she said soothingly, "Let's talk about your work . . ."

"BeeeeEEEEEEEP," said the machine as the bars almost jumped up off the screen.

"Okay," she said, "we'll get to that later. How about your family?"

"BeeeEEEEP," went the machine.

Presumably she didn't want to overload the machine, so we moved on to other topics, and did some "guided meditation." This consisted of imagining myself on a desert island. I had never been to a desert island, so I had a hard time visualizing this. Instead, I imagined myself on the Jersey shore, which seemed to work just as well. Then Anne mentioned, quite casually, that all of her patients also see her partner, a psychiatrist, named Dr. Tchachke. "Great," I said immediately, "when do I see him?" By now I was completely sold on therapy, so I gladly made an appointment to see him in a week.

Dr. Tchachke had a dark office filled with his own *tchachkes*, tall wicker baskets and, displayed on the wall, his diploma from the University of Pennsylvania. I ended up seeing Anne one week and Dr. Tchachke the next.

Dr. Tchachke was a good listener. I talked to him about everything: the stress I felt at work, my family, and how I felt trapped. We talked about my fears, my desires, my fantasies, and—despite some initial misgivings—my dreams and sexual fantasies. Though the sessions were clarifying, I was horrified that my life seemed to have no real order, no real purpose, and no real meaning for me. I was on an exceedingly dull treadmill, similar to the one I used every day in the company gym.

The logic of my life seemed depressingly circular: I work so that I can afford things like food and rent and clothes, so that I can live, so that I can work. It didn't seem at all fruitful. And it made no sense.

Therapy continued for a few months. It was strange; I knew that nothing was changing, but I seemed to see things more clearly. My stomach wasn't improving any, and I still felt stressed out, but at least I finally understood *why* I felt that way.

One chilly day in May, when it seemed as if we had gone over everything, Dr. Tchachke asked me, quite suddenly, "What would you do if you could do anything you wanted?"

"Oh that's easy," I blurted out. "I'd be a priest."

"Well, why don't you?" he asked.

Yeah, I thought, why *don't* I?

Suddenly it all made sense! I experienced a sense of blinding clarity that was, to put it mildly, new to me. I *did* want to become a priest. I wasn't sure of all the reasons, and maybe the reasons I was sure of weren't even the best ones. Maybe I wanted to escape, maybe I wanted others to respect me, and maybe I wanted to play martyr. But along with those reasons were other, deeper ones. I wanted to serve God and other people. I wanted to live the kind of life that Thomas Merton lived—even though I didn't much understand it. I wanted to feel the calm that he felt when he entered the monastery. I loved going to church; I felt at home there. I felt a real desire to become a priest and the rightness of the pull. The one thing, I realized, that had held me back for the last two years was worrying about what others would think or that maybe I was entering for the wrong reasons. Earlier that week, I had run across these lines by the novelist Louis Auchincloss:

> Oh, how obvious these conclusions seem! And yet a man can spend his whole existence never learning the simple lesson that he has only one life and that if he fails to do what he wants with it, no one really cares.

I went home that day in May of 1988 and fished from my desk the stuff the Jesuits had sent me two years ago. How could I have been so blind? I *wanted* to do this like nothing else. And I wanted to do it *now*.

I riffled through the few cream-colored letters that I had kept. Most of them said things like "We're having another meeting of men interested in the Jesuits. Why don't you come?" Or, "We haven't heard from you recently." (That was exceedingly polite, I thought, given that I had torn up most of their letters.) And, "Let us know if you still want to be on our mailing list." Eventually, the letters had stopped.

The next day at work I closed my door and called the Jesuit in charge of recruiting, or "vocations." There was a new man on the job named Fr. Jim Kane.

He called me back at work the next day. It was an auspicious time to talk to the Jesuits.

EARLIER IN THE week, Karen had handed me a short list of GE employees that she had received from her manager. She told me to contact the people on the list to find out if they were interested in applying for a job in our division. She also wanted me to call their managers to "clear" them, that is, to ensure they were available to interview for a new job. As it turned out, no one was interested. By the time I had finished contacting all of the employees and their managers, the list was crowded with phone numbers, notations, markings, and check marks.

A few days later I got a call from a guy who identified himself as Mike Smith. (Again, out of charity, I've changed the
names.) That was the only identification he gave, other than to
say he was the manager of one of the employees on the list.
Why hadn't I contacted him directly? he wanted to know. I
looked through my files, found the list, and glanced down at my
scribblings. Next to his employee's name I had written "Bob"
and a check mark.

"Well, it looks like I spoke with someone named . . . Bob,"
I said. "But in any event the employee wasn't interested in the
job. At least that's what I have written down. Is there a problem? Did I call the wrong person?"

"Next time just call me directly," said Mike, somewhat
icily. "Okay?"

"Okay," I said, figuring that was that.

It was not.

The next day, after I stuffed the list back in my file cabinet,
I got a call from my manager. "Come in here right now," she
said. Karen sounded annoyed. But then again, she frequently
sounded annoyed.

She was standing, red-faced, behind her desk. Before I said
anything she shouted, "Did you talk to Mike Smith? He just
called me."

Initially, I was happy that I had *already* talked to Mike and
had cleared everything up. I already had the answer to my manager's question—something that we were taught was the hall-
mark of a good employee.

So I said proudly, "Mike wondered if I had talked to the
right person to clear an employee in his division. I looked at my
list and told him the name of the manager I contacted. And I
told Mike that I would contact him in the future if we ever
needed one of his guys." I thought I had handled his questions
perfectly—especially the part about promising to call him in
the future. I awaited praise.

Karen slammed her hand down on her desk. "He says
you're a *liar!*"

She informed me that this Bob denied *ever* talking to me.
Now, either my notes were wrong, or Bob was trying to save

his neck if he had forgotten to inform Mike, his own manager. Either way, all Mike had to do was call back and explain the confusion to me. But this being GE, he didn't. Instead, he called my managers and called me a liar. And worse, it now turned out that Mike was *president* of one of GE's largest divisions (he never gave his job title over the phone), and thus one of the most powerful men in the entire company.

"He has gone to my boss and asked that you be fired for lying!" said my manager.

"Lying!" I shouted, astonished and beginning to grow angry. "My God, I thought I had cleared everything with the right guy. I mean, I still think I did! And I told him in the future that I would call him directly!"

"You're a *liar!*" Karen said.

"But there's a big difference between making an honest mistake and trying to deceive someone!"

"You're a liar!"

I could feel my face flushing.

"At least let me call him and . . . "

"No. You will *not!*" she shouted. "You've already done *enough* damage. I will *not* tolerate liars on my staff."

It got worse. Karen refused to listen to me; her boss thought I was lying, too. Didn't division heads like Mike have anything better to do than to try to get me fired from my job? Apparently not.

I stuck by my story: even if I had made a mistake, it was an honest mistake and I hadn't set out to deceive anyone. (I never even suggested that the other guy might be lying to save his neck.) I certainly had nothing to gain by making something up. It was all so confusing, and I left the office close to tears. To me, the episode pretty well encapsulated life at GE.

ALL OF THIS was on my mind when Father Kane called me back. So were my thoughts about vocation. I closed the door to my office.

"Hi. Thanks for returning my call," I said. "I'm interested in joining the Jesuits."

"Well," said Fr. Kane, "that's great." Did this mean I was in? "We'll send you some information so you can start attending our candidates' meetings. It's too late for this year, but we'll start thinking about applying for next year. We've already accepted our incoming class for August."

Next year? I certainly did not want to wait another year. I was ready now. Never having had any firsthand experience with Jesuits or, for that matter, any religious order, I approached the delay much the same way that I would one at work: as an obstacle to be surmounted by sheer force of will.

"Oh no," I told him, "I want to enter *this* year. I've already decided. Next year just is too far away. Let's shoot for this August, okay?"

Though I could tell he was a bit taken aback, he took my response in stride. "I'll be in Fairfield for a wedding next week," he said. "Why don't we chat then?"

Great. Something inside me clicked and I shifted into high gear. I also made an appointment to see the vocation director at the diocesan seminary in Philadelphia. I figured if I was going to do this, I might as well cover all the bases.

I still hadn't told anyone about my plans. Though I was excited about the idea of joining the Jesuits, my embarrassment remained. The first person I confided in was my friend Bruce, whom I saw frequently enough that denial would have been difficult if not impossible. One Saturday, we were driving around aimlessly and ended up at an outdoor sculpture museum in Orange County, north of New York City, called Storm King. Appropriately enough, it looked like a thunderstorm would break at any minute. I decided it would be a good time to tell him.

To my great surprise, he said, "That sounds like a good idea." Since he had attended a Jesuit high school and certainly knew more about the Jesuits than I did, he was able to ask a few informed questions.

"Will they send you overseas?" No, I don't think so.

"How long before you're ordained?" Ten years.

"Won't your parents hit the roof?" Probably.

"When would you leave GE?" Probably in a few months.

He mulled this over for a few seconds. "Good," he said. "You never belonged there anyway." And hearkening back to the sermons we heard in college, he smiled and said, "Now, Jim, as a good Catholic, I have to ask you: What's in this for me? What do *I* get out of your joining the Jesuits?"

A few weeks later I finally screwed up my courage and decided to tell my family. I had no idea how they would react. My parents were still separated, so I knew that any important news would undoubtedly provoke a strong reaction. Though no one in my family was particularly "religious," at least in the sense of being ardent, churchgoing Catholics, I held out some hope that they would be pleased.

I told Carolyn first, so that she could comfort my mother about the impending tragedy.

"The Jesuits?" she exclaimed. "The priesthood?"

Of course she was surprised. I had had a few years to get used to the idea, and was now giving her a few seconds. Carolyn cried as she asked whether or not I would be able to have a family, if I would have to move, if she would be able to see me. She said she thought that priests were overworked and lonely. She cried some more. But she recovered quickly, and started asking questions that made me glad that I had told her.

"You always did look good in black," she said finally.

By a stroke of unfortunate timing, I told my mother on Mother's Day. And since, like my sister, she had no clue that I was planning on altering my life so radically, she was very upset—to put it mildly—and cried profusely. She was particularly sad that I wasn't going to have any children, and worried that I would never see her again. Though I could certainly understand her concerns, her reaction made me less comfortable and confident about what I was doing. Fortunately, my sister was on hand to help her adjust to the news.

Even though I was convinced that I wanted to join the Jesuits, I thought it would be good to check out, as it were, the competition—the diocesan clergy. They had a lot of things in their favor. First, the training wasn't nearly as long (five years compared to the Jesuits' ten) and, second, I wouldn't be bouncing around from place to place like I would be with the Jesuits. I would be rooted in one diocese, in this case Philadelphia. Maybe this would make my family happier. I called the St. Charles Borromeo Seminary to schedule an interview. Vocations to the priesthood being as they were in those days, they were more than happy to arrange one.

The Friday before the interview at St. Charles, I stopped in New York to visit my sister, who had by then graduated from Harvard and was living on the Upper East Side. Before dropping by her apartment, I stopped by a religious bookstore in her neighborhood. I thought perhaps they might carry books with titles like *So You Want to Be a Jesuit* or maybe even *So Your Son Wants To Be a Jesuit*. While the information the Jesuits had given me was helpful, I needed to know more. Although they didn't have those particular titles, I found some books on the priesthood that looked useful.

When Carolyn and I left her apartment, we discovered that everything had been stolen from the trunk of my car: a new grey Brooks Brothers suit; an expensive pair of new shoes; and all of my just-purchased books on the priesthood. Surely this meant something. Maybe it was a sign . . . but of what? Should I take this as a sign that I should let go of material possessions and embrace a life of poverty in the Jesuits? Or perhaps instead of thinking and reading about a vocation, I should just pray about it. Perhaps this was why the books were stolen. Or perhaps this was a sign that the visit to the diocesan seminary was a bad idea? Or was the whole idea of the priesthood wrong? I pondered this great mystery.

"I think it's a sign all right," Carolyn commented. "It's a sign you should get a better lock for your trunk."

Saint Charles Borromeo Seminary is located in Philadelphia on a large, wooded plot across from the archbishop's baronial residence on City Line Avenue. The enormous main building boasts thick stone pillars holding up a portico over the entrance; inside are clean marble floors and wide, echoing corridors: The Church Triumphant. I bet they didn't hold hands during the "Our Father" here.

The seminary's director of vocations was named Father Flanagan. The Friday prior, my secretary had handed me a note saying in big letters, "Fr. Flanagan called." At the bottom she wrote, "Does Boys' Town want you back?" By this point, I had clued her in on the reason for his call. She took the news with equanimity, saying only that anything would be more fun than working for GE.

Father Flanagan was an amiable sort, whose one oddity was that he wore the style of patent-leather shoes favored by U. S. Marines and the Philadelphia Police Department, the kind that could be shined with Windex. Would I have to wear those shoes? I wondered. I noticed right away that the seminarians wore cassocks. Cool. I imagined myself in a cassock, hands clasped behind my back, thinking about weighty theological questions as I strolled under the tall maple trees of St. Charles. It certainly beat getting called a liar by managers at GE.

We chatted for about an hour about the application process (which seemed remarkably simple) and the five years of theology and philosophy. I was surprised that seminarians were expected to work during the summer, which rather destroyed my fantasy of locking myself away while the world looked on in silent respect. (Somehow, a seminarian working during the summer I found unseemly. Such was my well-informed conception of the priesthood.)

I went back to my parents' house that day and lay outside on a lawn chair in our backyard, reading another Thomas Merton book. My mother came up to me and asked me how it went. "Great!" I said. I could really see myself being happy at St. Charles. My family was certainly more enthusiastic about the idea of my joining the diocesan seminary after they learned it was a shorter program than the Jesuits and would keep me closer to home. They didn't much like the idea of the priesthood, but if I had to be a priest, I might as well stay close to home.

So it was with some ambivalence that I showed up for the Jesuit interview the following Monday at Fairfield University. In case anyone were to glance at my appointment book in my office, I had written: "Doctor's Appointment." Not that people were in the habit of snooping through datebooks, but I wanted to take no chance that anyone would find out prematurely, especially if things didn't work out.

It was 2:00 in the afternoon when I met Jim Kane, the vocations director. He had just come from a wedding and was wearing his Roman collar underneath a sweater vest and sports coat. He did not have patent-leather shoes. Jim was a young-looking forty, with reddish hair and an easy manner. We met in a musty old parlor in the Jesuit Community, with the worn rugs and uncomfortable furniture that I would later discover to be the hallmarks of Jesuit interior design.

He told me right away that I would have to postpone applying until next year. I therefore decided that it was my job to convince him otherwise during the next hour. I figured I certainly had enough experience interviewing and being interviewed in the past few years to be able to do so. This, however, would not be a typical interview.

After some small talk, he asked: "Who is God for you?"

Now *there* was a question I hadn't heard in any interviews at Wharton. (Unless, of course, the answer was supposed to be "Salomon Brothers.")

Let's see . . . God? I tried to recall my C.C.D. lessons.

"God," I said finally, "is the creator of the universe."

"Okay. Good." I could tell that I hadn't impressed him. "Can you talk to me about Jesus? Who is Jesus for you?"

Ha! A trick question. "Well, they're the same, right?"

"Okay," he said shifting in his seat, "let's talk about your work."

And we did, for a few minutes, then about my family, my hopes, my dreams, my fears. Conversation grew easier as I grew less concerned with impressing him and eventually I opened up. I talked about my frustrations at work, my disappointment in what I was doing with my life and, finally, the most important part of my life: how I didn't seem to be able to shake the desire to be a Jesuit.

"I want to do it more than anything else. Does that make any sense?" He said that it did.

In the middle of all of this, he said, "If it's not too personal, Jim, I'd like to talk about your sex life." (How much more personal you could get?) And we did. But not being comfortable with talking about any of that, I took the easy way out and told him what I thought he wanted to hear. Lied, that is. That I was not a virgin (I was) and that I was completely comfortable with chastity (which I certainly wasn't).

Then he asked me: "Do you masturbate often?"

Here was *definitely* a new interview question. It took me aback initially, but later made me realize that the Jesuits were at least honest about human sexuality. (After the interview, a friend at GE laughingly suggested an answer to his question: "That depends. How many times a day do you consider often?")

Then it was my turn. I asked all the questions that had been bottled up in my mind for two years: What was it like being a Jesuit? How could you be sure that you had a "vocation"? What would my life be like as a Jesuit? And the smaller, but no less pressing questions: Would I be able to see my friends and family? (Of course, he said.) Would I have any say in what I did after ordination? (Yes, and even before ordination.) Would I really have to go to the Third World in novitiate? (Yes.)

Finally, did I have to wait a whole year?

He considered this for what seemed like a full minute. "Well, let's see what I can do."

So at least I had a shot for this year.

Based on the interview, I thought that the Jesuits were, in GE lingo, a better "fit" than St. Charles Borromeo. Though I thought I might be a good parish priest, I kept coming back to the fact that you could do almost anything in your life as a Jesuit. You could be a Jesuit teacher, a Jesuit artist, a Jesuit architect, a Jesuit missionary. (Father Kane cheerfully told me that there were even Jesuit accountants who helped keep the books, but I hoped I wouldn't have to do that.)

I could hardly design a better life; it seemed ideal. This, I was told later, is what's known by priests and sisters as "first fervor," that is, the feeling that religious life is almost perfect. Of course it's a naïve notion. But it's fun while it lasts.

When I returned to work that day, I told my secretary that I had learned some new interview questions to ask in the future.

In a few weeks, Fr. Kane telephoned to say that the Society would "consider" me for this year, as unusual as this was. But it would take a lot of work on my part. I would have to fill out a lengthy application, write an autobiography, get seven recommendations, go through a series of psychological tests in Boston, and interview with six or seven Jesuits in New England. Finally, I would have to make an eight-day retreat with a Jesuit.

The application was remarkably short. Ten pages of detailed questions about your background, parents, education, and some easy questions about why you wanted to enter the Society, all on eight or nine sheets of pale green paper. The autobiography, however, needed to be in greater detail. I finished both of them in a few days and, like any good young executive, Fed-Exed them to Boston. Then I distributed my recommendation forms to six friends, three from work and three from school. And one for my mother who, despite her initial hesitancy, told the Jesuits (as she does everyone) how wonderful I was. Some instincts are stronger than others. Next came the interviews.

A Father Higgins, one of the vice presidents at Fairfield University, was my first interviewer. I waited in the Administration Building, Bellarmine Hall, a sprawling Tudor-style mansion that had once served as the Jesuit Community. I think Fr. Higgins recognized that I was new to all of this Jesuit stuff, or perhaps he had been tipped off, because the interview was very relaxed and informal. He first asked how I had gotten interested in religious life.

Since I still didn't know whether or not Thomas Merton was well known, I said tentatively, "I read this book called *The Seven Storey Mountain* . . . by someone named Thomas Merton." He smiled.

"Have you heard of it?" I asked politely.

"Yes. I really enjoy Thomas Merton's writings." Then he said, without any condescension or pride, "In fact, I've written a book about him, on his idea of prayer." He reached behind him and pulled it out of a bookcase.

"Wow, *cool!*" I thought, and said.

We talked about Thomas Merton for a long while: about his life, his writing, his spirituality. And I found out some new things that one couldn't discover from reading his autobiography. I was impressed with the Jesuit who sat in front of me. I had certainly never met anyone who had written a book, and found it the height of sophistication. But far more appealing was the way this very learned man spoke, that is, naturally and without making me feel like I was being talked down to.

The Jesuits I met during the interviews were terribly accomplished. They all seemed to have graduate degrees, which were mentioned only in passing, if at all. They taught theology, psychiatry, philosophy, mathematics; they had written articles and books; they had worked in Brazil, Sudan, Jamaica, Iraq. They had founded schools, started retreat houses, and ran parishes. None of them was in any way condescending or imperious. In fact, the provincial was the most enjoyable one of all. It was quite the opposite of the Jackass Theory I learned at GE. The "higher" I got in the Jesuit hierarchy, the nicer they seemed to get.

No one laughed or raised an eyebrow when I described my lack of Catholic "education," or the fact that I didn't have many Catholic friends, or that I had never really done many "good works." All things that I thought might torpedo my chances of being accepted.

Belatedly, I thought I had better investigate other religious orders. The proximate occasion for this was receiving in the mail a sort of catalog describing a great variety of religious orders. Each religious order had a small advertisement and a card to clip out and mail. The afternoon I received it, I called Bruce to ask what he knew about the orders in the book. Since he had gone to a Jesuit high school, he was the expert.

I cradled the phone on my shoulder and flipped through the book.

"Here's one," I said. "The Order of St. Joseph."

"What do they do?" Bruce asked.

"They work in Africa."

"Oh well, forget about *that*," he said.

"Okay, how about, wait a minute . . . the Order of the Paraclete?"

"The *Parakeet?*"

"No," I said. "Paraclete."

"Well forget that. Everyone will think it's 'parakeet' for as long as you're in. What do they do anyway?"

"Um," I read the description. "They take care of priests."

"Now, that's interesting," he said. "See if you can find the order of priests they take care *of* and join *them*."

At work, I was by now fielding a lot of calls from the Jesuits, and felt guilty about working at GE and considering the Society of Jesus at the same time. But at this point there was little else I could do. I certainly couldn't announce that I was leaving, since I wasn't sure if the Jesuits would even accept me. I figured I'd just let everyone remain curious.

In the middle of June, I drove to Boston for my psychological tests. The tests, administered by a psychiatrist retained by the Jesuits, were conducted in a large, concrete bunker-like building, near the old Boston Garden.

The first obstacle was a Rorschach test, which Bruce and I had enjoyed taking at Penn. Unfortunately, all of the pictures looked like vaginas or bats to me. Not wanting to advert to the former, I kept saying, "That's a bat."

"Another bat."

"A bat."

"Um, a bat."

I realized this was sounding morbid. I felt like someone from *The Addams Family*. Doubtful that the Jesuits would accept someone who saw bats in every picture, I switched to something more cheerful.

"A butterfly."

"Oh, another butterfly . . . " and so on, for the remainder of the test.

The next task was to describe a picture. The doctor showed me a drawing of a girl leaning against a tree, holding some books in her arms, and looking forlornly into the distance. Behind her, two older people bent down to work in some sort of garden. "Now, can you come up with a story to match the picture?" asked the doctor.

"This girl is interested in leaving home," I said. "She feels it's time to leave, but she's really upset because she thinks she needs to stay behind to help her parents, who are having a hard time on the farm. They would really rather that she didn't go away and . . ."

Horrified, I stopped. I was telling *my* story, not hers, which I guessed was the insidious aim of this particular test.

I looked up at the psychiatrist. "Yes?" he said, smiling. "Go on."

This was awful. I had better think quickly or they'll *never* let me in. It sounds too depressing.

"Finally, though, her parents say it's okay for her to leave, and she moves away and is very happy." I smiled. The doctor looked annoyed.

Next he introduced the "general intelligence" part of the test. "When was Goethe born?" he asked. "How far is it from LA to New York?" The questions from the psychological tests at Penn that Bruce and I had researched! I answered all of the questions, happy that my college education had paid off. It couldn't hurt, I reasoned, if the Jesuits thought I was some sort of supergenius. And it must have surprised the examiner that there was someone walking around with the birth date of Goethe in his head.

Finally, I ran through the Minnesota Multiphasic Personality test. It lasted three hours and included questions like:

I appear on major magazine covers each week. True/False
I feel a tight band around my head. True/False
Dogs laugh at me. True/False

(Later my sister asked what would happen if you actually *had* appeared on several magazine covers and answered "yes."

Apparently, it would be difficult for celebrities to enter the Jesuits.)

The whole ordeal, which lasted around four or five hours, drained me. Afterwards Jim Kane drove me to the Jesuit novitiate in Boston, which they called Arrupe House, to spend the night.

Like a number of American novitiates, Arrupe House was a former convent. The novices lived in the Jamaica Plain neighborhood of Boston, sandwiched between the housing projects populated mainly by African-Americans and the mostly Hispanic section of the neighborhood. A few months prior to my visit, the Jesuits of New England had decided to move their novitiate from Newbury Street in downtown Boston, a neighborhood that became too swank to pretend that the novices were living anywhere near or among "the poor." On Friday and Saturday nights you could hear *salsa* music from passing cars, punctuated by an occasional scream or gunshot. The convent had been abandoned for a few years after the sisters had moved out. And, since the local parish had insufficient resources to care for it, it was pretty decrepit when the Jesuits asked to rent and renovate it.

The novitiate itself was an imposing four-story brick building with a large living room, an enormous kitchen, a bright, airy dining room, a TV room, a laundry, about twenty-five tiny bedrooms (apparently the nuns didn't need a lot of space), and a large number of bathrooms (a number which would seem even larger when, as a novice, I would have to clean them). On the second floor was the novitiate library with floor-to-ceiling bookcases and a huge oak trestle table brought from the old novitiate on Newbury Street. On the third floor, besides the novices' tiny bedrooms, was a plain, high-ceilinged chapel; its rough, stucco walls were painted a pale green, and a large wooden cross hung behind a simple oak altar. The fourth floor had the rest of the community's bedrooms and a few rooms for guests.

I was greeted by the novice director, named Jerry, and his assistant, David, both of whom seemed startlingly normal and terribly friendly. The few other novices I met that night were genial—and not at all what I had expected. Though by now I had met a few other Jesuits, I still expected ascetic-looking young men, hands clasped behind their backs, who would greet me saying something like, "We are so pleased that God has called you. Shall we pray?"

Instead, the novices were interested in how my application process was going. They also gave me small *précis* on each of the men with whom I still had to interview. We talked about the psychological tests I had taken earlier in the day. "Did they show you pictures of the vaginas?"

As much as I liked the idea of strolling around the sylvan grounds of St. Charles Borromeo in my black cassock, I liked Arrupe House even more. If it was less romantic (no cassocks, no marble halls, for that matter no marble anything) it seemed more comfortable. On the other hand, I wondered, did these guys pray much? Not that *I* did, but I was hearing enough about prayer that I was beginning to get the idea that it was an important thing to do.

My retreat was scheduled for three weeks later, at the beginning of June, at a Jesuit retreat house called Campion Center. To go, I would have to use up eight days of precious vacation time at GE. (My first actual sacrifice: vacation time.) And it was to be a *silent* retreat, much to the delight of my secretary, who asked me if I could remain silent for eight minutes, let alone eight days.

I called Jim Kane and asked him what the "agenda" was going to be. Perhaps, I suggested, he could fax it to me.

"There's really no agenda on a retreat," he said. "We just let God do the work."

Great, I thought, they don't have a clue.

Campion Center is located in Weston, a wooded suburb a few minutes outside of Boston, and up the street from Walden Pond and the towns of Lexington and Concord. It was originally the home of the old Jesuit theology school, or "theologate" in Jesuitese, as well as the "philosophate," and was built during the 1920s, when the Society not only expected but received entering novice classes of forty or fifty. The main building is a sprawling brick affair: long, wide corridors with countless rooms for the scholastics, brothers, and priests who at one time crammed into the place. In the center of the building is a large three-story rotunda with shiny marble floors and capped by a great green dome. On the first floor of the rotunda stood four larger-than-life statues of St. Ignatius Loyola, Mary, Jesus, and St. Joseph. The place smelled like every retreat house I have been in since—floor wax, soap, old carpets, candle wax, incense, and food.

The retreat center also serves as the New England province retirement home and as the province infirmary, where the older and more infirm Jesuits are resting or waiting to die, lending the site a slightly somber air.

Behind the main building, a gravel path, winding through a glade of evergreen trees, leads to the Jesuit cemetery. Row after row of Jesuits lie there, each plot marked with a simple granite headstone with the Jesuit's name inscribed in Latin above three dates: *Natus*, the birth date; *Ingressus*, the day the Jesuit entered the Society; and *Obiit*, the day he died. One night in 1956, the original New England novitiate in the Berkshire Mountains in western Massachusetts caught fire and burned to the ground while the community slept. The four Jesuits who died in that fire lie together in the cemetery in Weston.

The cemetery is impressive for its egalitarianism. All the Jesuits lie beneath identical grey tombstones, from scholastics who died before ordination to the oldest Jesuit missionary-archbishops. They lie side by side—theologians, retreat directors, college presidents, authors, teachers, pastors, bishops, cooks, novice directors, missionaries, artists, bookkeepers, porters, superiors, scholastics, saints, and sinners. This I found unaccountably and intensely moving.

In the middle of the building was a large chapel with a vaulted granite ceiling, an enormous white marble altar, and a black-and-white checkerboard marble floor. Running down both sides of the chapel were the smaller altars that were used when the priests who taught at the philosophate and theologate celebrated their "private Masses" each morning, assisted by a scholastic. Each side altar had a different name carved on its front: "Sacred Heart," "Saint Stanislaus," "Saint Ignatius." On each of the ornate stained glass windows, painted flowers and cherubs surrounded a single Latin word that represented one of the traditional fruits of the Holy Spirit: *Caritas, Gaudium, Patientia, Benignitas* . . .

In the stairways of Campion Center were tiny chapels—closets almost—each with its own private altar. The stout wooden doors had small peepholes cut in them. I found out later that these were sometimes used by recently ordained priests to practice their "rubrics," that is, their Mass technique. When an older father wanted to see if the chapel was occupied or perhaps if a young priest was saying his Mass correctly, he might peep in the hole and take a look.

The large dining room was divided into three parts by thick marble pillars that stretched to the twenty-foot ceiling. In the past, Jesuit philosophy students, theology students, and the fathers and brothers sat separately, according to their "grades." Fathers with fathers, brothers with brothers, scholastics with scholastics.

I was given a small room on the third floor, furnished in classic retreat-house style. A bed (single of course), a plain wooden desk, a sink, a metal chair, and a crucifix on the wall. My window overlooked a broad green meadow and, beyond, trees as far as the horizon. Directly beneath my window stood a white, weathered statue of St. Ignatius, left hand pointing skyward, right hand pointing to what looked from my window like a clipboard. (On closer inspection it turned out to be a book.) Near the other wing of the building stood a statue of St. Francis Xavier, the famous Jesuit missionary, likewise pointing to the heavens and holding a cross instead of a clipboard.

After exploring the building, I met with my retreat director, a recently ordained Jesuit named Ron, who had just finished a theology degree in Toronto. He quickly put me at ease and then asked me to spend some time "thinking" about who God was. The vocation director had asked me the same question, which I still thought was a pretty stupid one.

The next morning, after a big breakfast (in silence), I sat down in the chapel to come up with my list of who God was. Obvious: God was Creator, Giver of Life, All-Powerful, All-Good. I found the exercise tedious. So tedious, in fact, that my mind began to wander. I hoped that my list of God's attributes would be sufficiently correct. All the while I wondered: Is this prayer?

I spent the remainder of the day wandering around the town of Weston, lying out in the sun, and writing postcards to my friends.

When I saw Ron the next day, I dutifully enumerated my answers about God. I also admitted that I didn't seem to be able to focus on the assignment he had given me; my mind wandered too much. Maybe I wasn't cut out to be a Jesuit, I offered tentatively.

"That's okay," he said. "Don't concentrate next time. You can just let your mind wander. And think about this for a bit: *Who is Jesus?*"

Another dumb question.

So I walked around the grounds of the retreat center and thought about Jesus. Who *was* Jesus? Jesus was the Son of God, the Messiah, the Judge . . . all the things that I learned in Sunday school. Quickly I drew up another mental list.

Then I sat down on the warm grass and stopped thinking. I started to enjoy the day. Then very unexpectedly . . . *friend.* Jesus is also a friend, I thought.

Wow. Jesus is a friend. It felt pretty good to think of Jesus as a friend, a companion. I had never thought about it like that before. And it made me happy to think about Jesus in that way. So I lay back, looked up at the cloudless sky, and just enjoyed that thought. It would be great to be with Jesus, to have him accompany me, to be able to rely on him as I would rely on a good friend.

The next day I returned to the director and presented him with my list. I had written it down so I wouldn't forget. Jesus was the Son of God, Messiah, Judge.

And then, almost as an afterthought, I said, "You know, I had the funniest thought. The word *friend* just came into my mind. And I thought of how good it would be to have Jesus as a friend, you know, like a companion, someone you could talk to. I had a good time thinking about what that would be like."

Ron leaned back in his chair, smiled, and said, "I think you're beginning to pray."

It was a wonderfully liberating moment. He wasn't telling me that what I had experienced was right or wrong or rational or irrational or even Jesuit or not Jesuit. Instead, he was telling me—for the first time in my life—that it was okay to feel things about God, not just think them.

The structure of the retreat was appealing, everything was so orderly and peaceful. Maybe this is what life in a monastery was like, I thought, and realized why Thomas Merton would have felt so drawn to it. Breakfast, a meeting with my spiritual director, free time, lunch, daily Mass, more free time and, finally, dinner.

Most of the free time was given over to wandering the grounds and, especially, to prayer. Ron asked me to imagine Jesus in various scenes from the New Testament. Then I would try to place myself somewhere in the scene and let my mind wander. Essentially, he had taken what I thought was a weakness—an overly active imagination and a wandering mind—and was helping me use it to experience God in a new way. I found that I could imagine scenes from the Gospels fairly easily: people's faces, their clothes, their voices, the smells of the place, the sounds, the landscape, the buildings. And when I had envisioned the whole scene and finally imagined myself therein, I was often surprised by my feelings and reactions. Sometimes I felt happy to be with Jesus, or, like his disciples, surprised and confused by his actions or words. Praying like this made me feel closer to God.

At the end of the retreat, we returned to my image of Jesus as a companion. "By the way," Ron said, "it might interest you to know that the original name of the Society of Jesus is the Company—or Companions—of Jesus." Wow. For someone looking for signs, it seemed to be an important, albeit small one, that I was headed in the right direction.

After the retreat Jim Kane drove me to the Jesuit ordinations at the College of the Holy Cross in Worcester, Massachusetts. This was my first official Jesuit function, so I was quite apprehensive. There was an official "candidates" meeting, where we watched a particularly cheesy video about the Jesuits in the U.S. While most of the applicants had spent a year or two attending these informational meetings, this was my one and only candidate meeting. (A few years later, after I had spoken to a group of candidates in Chicago, one guy asked me, "Did you use to like candidates meetings?" "Well, to be honest," I said sheepishly, "I didn't go to that many." "Yeah," he said. "Who wants to hang out with people who can't make up their minds!")

An ordination is one of the Catholic Church's best shows. And on that humid June day at Holy Cross they did it exceedingly well. First came a long procession of around one hundred Jesuit priests, wearing white vestments, filing into the ornate barrel-vaulted chapel, accompanied by booming organ music and a choir. They were followed immediately by the smiling priests-to-be, the *ordinandi*, dressed in white albs and the diagonal stole of the deacon. Finally the "ordaining prelate" entered, the archbishop dressed in alb, chasuble, stole, and miter. He carried his crozier and blessed people as he slowly made his way up the aisle. Add to this a dozen or so young Jesuit scholastics serving as acolytes, candle bearers, and a young novice swinging a censer, from which poured forth clouds of sweet incense. And this was only the first ten minutes.

It is a lengthy, ancient ceremony. After the Gospel was read, the bishop, seated under the enormous *baldachino* of the church, called out the names of the *ordinandi*, who answered, "I am ready and willing!" The Jesuit provincial then read a formal document attesting that, after long years of training, the men standing before the bishop had been judged worthy of ordination. The bishop then proclaimed his own approval: "We rely on the help of God and the Lord Jesus Christ, our Savior, and choose these men, our brothers, for the order of the priesthood." At this the congregation burst into a sustained applause. Following this, in a gesture that I found unaccountably moving, the *ordinandi* lay prostrate in the aisle of the church, in a gesture of humility. As they lay there, the organ breathed its deep voice over the congregation, and the choir began to chant the long prayer known as the Litany of the Saints.

"Holy Mary, Mother of God," sang the choir.

"Pray for us!" the people sang.

"Saint Michael . . . "

"Pray for us!"

"Saint Joseph . . . "

"Pray for us!"

When the men rose from the aisle, I noticed that many of them were weeping.

At the actual moment of ordination, the bishop, in a symbol stretching back to the time of the apostles, silently laid his hands on the heads of the men who knelt before him. All of the Jesuit priests in the church, in single file, then approached the men and followed the bishop's lead, laying their hands on the heads of the new priests. After this, the newly ordained removed their deacon stoles and put on the vestments of a priest. The bishop then anointed their hands with fragrant holy oil. Finally, after the rituals of ordination were completed, the bishops and the newly ordained celebrated a regular Mass.

The Ordination Mass lasted almost two hours. Entirely overwhelmed by its beauty, I was surprised to find tears streaming down my own face at its conclusion.

During the recessional hymn, as they walked out of the church into the bright sunlight, the new priests looked ecstatic. I thought of how fulfilling it must be for them after so many years of preparation. If I could have, I would have stayed with the Jesuits and ditched GE right there.

After the Mass, Jim informed me that the Society would not be able to come to any decision about my application until August 15. But entrance day was only two weeks after that—August 28. Not only would I have to wait a few more months to find out about my application, but the two weeks in between wouldn't leave me much time to prepare for a move. But I went back to Stamford more anxious than ever to join the Jesuits.

5.

The Sign of Jonas

*Like the prophet Jonas, when God ordered him to go to
Nineveh, I found myself with an almost uncontrollable desire
to go in the opposite direction. God pointed one way and all
my "ideals" pointed in the other. It was when Jonas was
traveling as fast as he could away from Nineveh, toward
Tharsis, that he was thrown overboard, and swallowed by a
whale who took him where God wanted him to go.*

Thomas Merton, *The Sign of Jonas*

It would, I realized, be impossible to wait until August 15 to
find out the Jesuits' decision, and then simply quit my job. I
couldn't give such short notice and just leave, without spending
a few weeks helping to recruit and train my replacement.
Instead, I would have to make a decision: Should I leave my job
before I knew whether the Jesuits had accepted me?

At the time, I expected a dramatic, incontrovertible answer
to this dilemma. In other words, a sign. I figured if I was com-
mitting my life to God, God could at least provide me with
something more tangible. But after a week of frustrating indecision, nothing came: no definite answer, no voices, no visions,
no warm feelings. Of course, if any of those things *had* happened, I probably would have been scared to death. Still, I
began to wonder if the experiences of the retreat—Jesus being
my friend and all the rest—had been an illusion.

The next Sunday I found myself in another church in Stamford, St. Mary's. During the Mass I prayed for a sign, something

that would help me see what I had to do. After Mass, out of desperation, I knelt in front of a statue of Jesus. I was so frustrated; hot tears filled my eyes. I prayed and said, "Take me!" as hard as I could. And suddenly I felt a wordless voice within me saying, "I will." It was unlike anything I had experienced. I had *felt* the words inside my head. Surprised, and a little frightened, I stood up immediately and bolted out of the church. Had I imagined the whole thing? I wasn't sure . . . I didn't think so. But what I *didn't* imagine was the sense of clarity about what I needed to do.

The answer was now obvious: yes, of course, quit work. Though it was willfully illogical—how could you quit a job without the promise of something else?—I figured that if I weren't accepted I could do some other work of some sort. I had a laughably dim idea that I could teach in a Catholic school somewhere, despite knowing less than the average sixth grader about Catholicism.

I gave my notice the next day. I sat down in Karen's office and explained that I was leaving, to become a priest.

"You're kidding, right?" she said.

After I assured her that I was not kidding, she asked me if I could stay to help her find someone. Then she thought for a minute and said, "Wow! Could you baptize children?" I guessed so. "Great. Maybe you could baptize mine?" Sure, I said, why not?

After six years at GE, it was difficult to believe that I could give it all up so readily. But the intense desire to enter the Jesuits made leaving the company easier. I knew that I would miss my coworkers but, by this point, not the work. And the more I thought about it, the more I couldn't wait to enter the novitiate.

I had enormous fun spreading the news. By this time my secretary was calling me "Father Martin" and I felt great about the whole thing—a bit pious, basking in the glow of The Man Who Gave It All Up. But underneath that vanity was a real sense of relief and excitement, even joy.

When I had left for the retreat I hadn't told anyone, other than my secretary, where I was going. After I returned from

Boston, my friends at work were more than a little curious about where I had disappeared to. "Where *were* you?" my friend Kate asked at 9:00 on Monday morning.

"Let's have lunch, and I'll tell you." I said. "Bring along Chris and Chip, too. I have some news for you."

Such a mysterious response, I knew, would guarantee their presence at 12 noon in my office.

"I have something to tell you," I said after I shut the door.

"You're leaving GE!" they shouted in unison. (Apparently I was less successful than I thought in hiding my unhappiness with work.)

"That's the easy part," I said. "Now you have to guess why."

"You're moving back to Philadelphia," said Chris.

"No."

"You're going to get your M.B.A."

"Oh God," I groaned, "no way."

This continued for a few minutes.

"Give up?" I asked. They nodded.

"I'm joining the Jesuits."

Silence and puzzled glances.

"Isn't that . . . , " said Kate tentatively. "I think that's like a priest . . . isn't it?"

"Yup," I said.

Kate jumped out of her chair, "You're *kidding!*"

Later that day, since I figured word would spread rapidly, I visited some other friends, most of whom also said some variation of "You're kidding." My friend Reid played the same guessing game, failing miserably. Finally, I told her and she jumped out of her chair and shouted, "You're *kidding!*" attracting the rest of her department, with whom I had to share my secret.

I couldn't wait to tell Rob, my old roommate, in person, so I phoned him at his office.

"A priest? You're kidding," he said. When I assured him that I was not, he said, "*Mazel tov!*" I mentioned that I thought it would be fun to tell the rest of our friends over dinner.

"Promise me you'll let me come," he said. "This I've got to see."

So I invited a few close friends from Penn to my favorite restaurant in Manhattan, called Le Brasserie, to spring the news on them. They were miffed at all the secrecy that I had intentionally let accompany the dinner. We sat down and I watched them squirm in anticipation. Finally, my friend Jim said, "Okay, Martin, what's going on?"

I said flatly, "I'm going to become a priest." All three of them said nothing for a good five seconds.

At that point the waiter arrived and asked us if we needed more time.

"Yes," said Andy, "we need a *lot* more time."

I swore them to secrecy until I could tell other friends face to face. I met with another friend from Penn, another Andy, now a lawyer. We went out to lunch.

"So are you going to tell me the big news that no one is willing to tell me?" he said right off.

"Okay. I'm going to become a Jesuit priest."

"What?" said Andy, incredulously.

I thought he might not have heard me. "I'm going to become a priest."

"What?" he said again.

"I'm going to become a priest."

"What?!"

"I'm going . . . "

"I heard you. You're what? Since *when?*" I explained the whole thing the best I could. That night, Andy would tell me later, he went home and looked up the definition of *Jesuit* in Webster's dictionary. He found:

> 1.) a member of the Society of Jesus, a Roman Catholic religious order for men, founded by Ignatius Loyola in 1534, and 2.) a crafty schemer; cunning dissembler; casuist; hostile and offensive term, as used by anti-Jesuits.

That the Jesuits were not as well known as I had thought would soon become evident. After I had patiently explained to another Jewish friend about my new course in life, he remarked, "I understand all the stuff about your wanting to become a priest, but I don't understand why you have to leave the Catholic Church to become a Jesuit." I endeavored to explain the situation again. "Are your parents Jesuits?" he asked.

Many of my friends thought I was running away. My standard response to this was that I was running *toward* something, not away from something. Which of course, was only partially true. Many of my GE friends suggested I slow down a bit. Was there really any need to enter right away?

What *was* I running away from? Family problems for one thing. I thought that by entering the novitiate, God would somehow take care of all of that, or at least make things better. I was definitely running from many of the things the corporate world stood for, at least in my own mind. The lack of compassion, the glorification of money and acquisitiveness, the emphasis on competition, the lack of respect for human dignity. But these were good things to run away from.

There was a "Peanuts" cartoon that shows Linus running away from home. "You can't run away from all of your problems," says Charlie Brown. "Why not?" answers Linus. "Well, what would happen if everyone ran away from their problems? Where would we be then?"

"At least we'd all be running in the same direction," says Linus.

MY LAST BIG responsibility before I left GE was to organize the department's annual picnic. Each year the company gave the finance staff a day off to enjoy a facsimile of what we used to call in elementary school "Sports Day." Planning the day required a lot of work—hiring caterers, finding a nearby country club that would allow hundreds of employees to descend on them *en masse*, deciding which sports to play and rounding up the equipment, sending out invitations and, finally, hiring a party-tent company to guard against inclement weather.

As a courtesy, I had sent an invitation to Dan at Corporate Headquarters, the "we-don't-owe-you-a-damn-thing" guy. No one in my department figured he would come because of his busy hi-pot schedule and, indeed, by the morning of the picnic he hadn't responded.

Everyone seemed to be in high spirits at the picnic. Volleyball and softball were selected as the day's sports, since even the athletically challenged could participate in volleyball and those who fancied themselves as athletes could opt for the more competitive softball games. Even the caterers were a big hit— an Italian restaurant in Stamford that specialized in meatball sandwiches, sausage subs, and hoagies. And it was a brilliantly clear day.

Towards the end of the day, though, it began to cloud over and, finally, drizzle. Soon, everyone was gathered under the yellow-and-white striped tents drinking sodas and finishing the last of the meatball subs. Though the invitation said that the picnic would end by 4:00, I let the party continue so we could polish off the rest of the food. At around 4:30, I told the caterers to start packing up, and grabbed my first sandwich of the day.

A few minutes later I was chatting with some friends, with a sandwich in one hand and a soda in the other. I noticed that they seemed to be staring over my shoulder and not paying particular attention to what I was saying.

"Is that *Dan?*" said one. "I thought you said he wasn't coming!"

I turned around just in time to see Dan emerge from a black stretch limousine that had arrived at the entrance to the country club. He extricated his portly body from the car and started walking towards us—across the now wet field—in a dark suit and tie. (The invitation had said "very casual," and the rest of us were wearing T-shirts and shorts.)

The conversation in the tent died down as Dan approached. He walked through the silent crowd and approached me. At least he knows me, I thought happily.

"Where's the food?" he said by way of greeting.

By now the caterers had loaded their steam tables and metal food trays back into their trucks. "Um, well, I think everything's already been put away," I said.

Karen, noticing Dan, had sidled up beside me. To express his displeasure that the food was gone, he glowered at us wordlessly.

"Jim, please get Dan some food," said my manager.

The only thing that the caterers hadn't yet spirited away was an ice cream cooler. I opened the lid and pulled out a Popsicle. My friends were watching this little drama with great fascination.

"You're going to give him a Popsicle?" said one, horrified, as I passed.

I saw his point and returned to Dan *sans* Popsicle. "Sorry, Dan," I offered, "but I don't think there's any food left. As it is, we already asked the caterers to stay longer than . . . "

"Great," he said testily.

And then, "Where are the damn *bathrooms* around here?"

Unhappily, the only bathroom was located in the clubhouse, a good hundred yards away, and it was now raining heavily. His face darkened when I told him this. "The only other alternative is a port-a-john," I pointed out. The port-a-john was closer to the tent but still required a walk across a wet field in the rain.

"Dammit," he said, and he started walking across the wet field in the rain, in his suit. Just then we heard a huge thunderclap and it started to pour.

Everyone in the tent watched Dan walk across the field, enter the port-a-john, emerge a few minutes later, and walk past the tent, across the parking lot and directly into the open door of his limousine, which promptly sped away. His entire visit had lasted about five minutes.

"If your career wasn't already over," said a friend to general laughter, "it would be now!"

A few days later, on the last day of July—coincidentally, the Feast of St. Ignatius of Loyola—my friends threw a going-away party for me in the cafeteria. By the time I left GE Capital, I had hired scores of people and helped dozens more find new positions, so I knew almost every employee. Though I felt certain about what I was doing, after six years with the same company, I left with mixed emotions. On the one hand, I was saddened by the thought of leaving so many friends behind. On the other, I was glad to escape from what I thought was an unhealthy environment. The Graphics Department presented me with a life-sized cartoon cutout of me in a monk's habit and cowl. Everyone signed it, penning in sarcastic remarks about poverty and chastity. I also made a little speech and shared with the crowd the new interview questions I had learned during my interviews with the Jesuits.

It seemed surreal. No job; no idea if I would even get into the Jesuits; no certainty at all, in fact, about what would come next. My friends, however, were surprised that I would worry about being accepted into the notiviate. "What are you talking about?" said Rob incredulously. "I'm sure they'll take you."

"You really think so?" I asked hopefully.

"Come on," he said, "I thought they were *desperate* for people."

To get my mind off the Jesuits I spent a few weeks with my friend Bruce visiting some of his friends in Seattle. When I confessed my nervousness, he repeated Rob's comment: "But aren't they *desperate?*"

BACK IN STAMFORD, on August 15, I got a phone call from Fr. Kane telling me that I had been accepted to the Society of Jesus. I was ecstatic; a whole new life was about to begin. I immediately called my family to tell them about the phone call. My mom was genuinely happy.

So was my sister. "Is this what they mean by 'getting the call'?" she asked.

Jim Kane called back a few minutes later to ask me some questions. I found out later that these are called "impediment questions." In other words, a "yes" to any of them would mean an impediment to ordination.

"Have you ever been married or fathered a child?" he asked blandly.

"*What?*" I said, genuinely surprised. "Don't you think I would have mentioned this in one of the eight zillion interviews I had?"

"I know," he answered. "I have to ask them anyway."

"No, I've never been married or fathered a child."

"Have you ever publicly repudiated the Church?"

"You mean like standing up during Mass and saying, 'I officially reject the Church'?"

"Something like that," he said.

"No."

"Have you ever murdered anyone?"

This was getting kind of silly, so I figured I'd have a little fun. "Hmm . . . murder? Well, it depends on what you mean exactly. Well, not exactly. At least not *technically*."

My answers having apparently presented no impediment, he said, "One more thing. The novice director in Boston has a list of items you need to bring, so you should talk with him."

"Okay," I said, lapsing back into my corporate-executive attitude. "Have him call me."

A few minutes later the novice director was on the line congratulating me. He also furnished me with a list of necessities. First, enough clothes to get me through two years. Second, a check for $250 to cover the cost of the vow ceremony in two years. Okay. Finally, a clerical shirt and a breviary. Right. Where do I buy a clerical shirt? And what's a breviary? A breviary is a prayer book, he explained. Go to any clerical goods store and they should have both of them. Tell them you want the *red* breviary. They'll know which one you mean, he said.

It was fortunate that he told me, since when I finally located a religious goods store in Philadelphia, they asked me which breviary I wanted. "The red one!" I blurted out. She smiled benignly, apparently having met one or two novices in her day, and handed it over. I flipped through it: apparently it was a book of prayers, psalms mostly, for different days of the week. It looked impressively pious; I felt holy just carrying it around.

I wasn't as lucky with the clerical shirt. After six years in business, I knew better than to buy anything other than one-hundred percent cotton Oxford-cloth shirts. But as far as clerical shirts went, there was nothing but a wide assortment of tacky polyester materials. Ugh. I started sweating just looking at the display in the store. I settled on a nice cotton-poly blend that already looked shiny.

I ran up to my room as soon as I got home and tore open the plastic wrapping. The white tab fit snugly into the black collar and, when I looked into the mirror, there I was: Father Martin!

Another item on the novice director's list was a pair of black pants, which is easy to find if you are not averse to having a grosgrain tuxedo stripe running down the side. The salesman at Jos. A. Banks in Stamford, where I had purchased at least a dozen suits over the past two years, asked why I suddenly needed black pants. "What, are you joining a seminary or something?" he laughed.

"Yes, actually I am." I said.

"Oh," he said quietly. "Please pray for me."

I also had to get rid of everything I owned. Well, more or less. Initially, I had notions of St. Francis, who brought all of his possessions to the public square in Assisi and burned them as a sign of his decision to commit all to God. My own distribution, however, would be somewhat less dramatic.

There were some things that I definitely wouldn't be needing at the novitiate. My car, my stereo, my tapes and records, my suits, a large collection of books. And I had to get rid of the apartment. Fortunately, the two roommates with whom I now lived, Ed and Peter, had by that time also had enough of GE; they too were leaving the area—one for graduate school and one for a job in Boston. The three of us had to clear out by the end of August.

We had a tough time finding someone to buy our ratty furniture. Surprisingly, Goodwill refused to accept any furniture and the Salvation Army dropped by our house, picked up a few pieces of furniture, and rejected the rest. Where were all those needy, furniture-less people?

I kept trying to find someone to take the remainder, when one Sunday Ed walked into the living room. "Good news!" he announced. "I found someone who wants our furniture."

"Great," I said, "How much?"

"Seventy-five bucks," he said.

"Great!"

"No," said Ed, sensing my confusion. "We pay *them* seventy-five bucks."

Francis of Assisi, I thought, probably couldn't have afforded to be poor today.

Bruce dropped by one day to picked through the few hundred books that I had in my room. "Not bad," he said as he carried out an armful of paperbacks to his car. "People should join the Jesuits more often." (I reminded him that he had at last found something in it for *him*.) My mom bought my Mazda for a dollar, to make it legal.

The weekend before I left, there was another going-away party, in Philadelphia, attended by friends from New York, Philadelphia, and D.C. My friend Mary came dressed in a clerical shirt (apparently *she* knew where to buy them) and presented me with a gift: a clear plastic statue of the Virgin Mary, with a plastic crown (a convenient screw-off one) which she had purchased at the Basilica of the Immaculate Conception in Washington. When not being used as an object for devotion, the Blessed Mother could be used to hold holy water.

My cousin Rosie made me a cake in the shape of a cross. I told her how clever it was to split two pound cakes like that. "Oh no," she protested, "this is a *mold*." A cross mold? How many times did she expect to use it? "Well, I've already used it for one confirmation, a first Communion, and today. So, that's three times in one year. Not bad, huh?"

She said she would save it for my ordination.

6.

The Manner Is Ordinary

*In other respects, for sound reasons and with attention
always paid to the greater service of God, in regard to what
is exterior the manner of living is ordinary.*

The Constitutions of the Society of Jesus

Traditionally, the Society of Jesus in the United States asks
its novices to begin their training as Jesuits in late August.
So on August 28, after I had quit my job, divested myself of at
least some of my worldly goods, and said my goodbyes, I
packed my bags and headed for the novitiate. My two roommates, Ed and Peter, along with Ed's girlfriend, Beth, drove
with me to Boston. My father, still separated from my mother,
flew in from the West Coast to drive up with my mother from
Philadelphia, picking up my sister in New York on the way.

After arriving at Arrupe House, my roommates and I
brought my stuff to my room. Since it was a former convent,
the rooms were large enough to accommodate only one bed
(twin, of course), a chair, and a desk. Alas, no closets. The nuns
had owned two habits—the one they wore and an extra one that
they hung on the back of the door. But, as an accommodation
to our more worldly wardrobes, we had the use of large
armoires that stood outside our rooms.

At 2:00 in the afternoon, a Mass was celebrated in the
small house chapel with our families and the other novices.

During Mass two friends arrived at the novitiate and kept ringing the bell, shouting from outside, "Jim! Is this the right place? Hello?" Someone eventually ran down three flights of stairs to let them in; they burst into the chapel sweaty and out of breath.

During the lunch that followed, I watched my parents and sister try to make some sense of the situation. They were all somewhat stressed to begin with, as this was the first time that my mother and sister had been with my father in a while. And they also tried, for my benefit, to portray an image of a good Catholic family. I overheard the novice director ask my sister where she lived. "New York," she replied.

"No kidding," he said. "Whereabouts?"

"East 84th Street," said Carolyn.

"Then you must be a parishioner at St. Ignatius," he said, referring to the Jesuit-run church only a few blocks from my sister's apartment. But I knew she rarely attended church there, or anywhere else for that matter.

"Uh, yeah . . . , " she said.

"Isn't the altar lovely?" asked the novice director.

"Uh, yeah, it sure is . . . "

Carolyn said later that she didn't want to embarrass me. She also met Tom, one of the second-year novices, who asked her how she had enjoyed the Catholic students' group at Harvard. (*Very* much, she replied cheerfully if not exactly truthfully.) But I appreciated the effort and understood the spirit in which it was offered.

My parents, particularly my mother, were also not used to being around so many clerics. "Which ones are priests?" she whispered during the afternoon. "Well," I said, "everyone who looks over forty is a probably a priest."

"You're kidding!" she said. "I called one of them by his first name!"

Around 3:00, my family left, in tears. I kissed them as I stood by their car and promised to call and write and generally keep in touch. As I watched their car drive away, I felt a sudden stab of fear. What had I gotten myself into?

The community had dinner a few hours later, after the new novices had finished unpacking their few things. Afterwards was a short meeting during which the novice director told us a lot of helpful pointers about the novitiate which, owing to my great anxiety, I promptly forgot.

Late that night, after I had crawled under the covers, worried and uncertain, I wept. Was I doing the right thing? The whole "Jesuit thing," as one of my friends called it, started to seem weird all over again.

BY DAYBREAK I felt much improved. The first day proved relaxing and I was reminded that everyone was pretty normal and nonthreatening. The basic rhythm of the novitiate, while not as leisurely as the rhythm I had enjoyed on retreat, was markedly slower than the pace at GE. The first two weeks were particularly relaxing. It was almost like being on vacation.

The first two weeks of novitiate are called "postulancy," a holdover from the times when incoming novices (at this point still "postulants" to the Society) found themselves on probation. Years ago, at the end of a Jesuit postulancy, as in most religious orders, you received your habit. In the case of the Jesuits, this meant receiving a long black cassock tied with a black sash around your waist. In some women's orders, at the end of the postulancy period, a postulant would return to her room to find on her bed either her habit or her old "street" clothes—thus communicating the decision of her superior.

In the New England novitiate, postulancy served instead as a sort of low-key introduction to the life of a novice. We learned about the daily and weekly schedule of the novitiate; the governance of the Society; the role of the novice director, his assistant, and other superiors; what we would do during the coming year; and—this I remember most—how to use the breviary. (It would take me almost the entire year to learn how to use it.)

At the end of the two weeks, the three first-year novices spent a weekend in Gloucester, Massachusetts, where the Jesuits run a delightful retreat house on Cape Anne. It's an extremely popular place for retreats, mainly because of the spectacular scenery: the house is perched on a rocky peninsula above the Atlantic. Looking through the plate-glass windows in the dining room you can watch the ocean change colors: pale grey in the morning, steel blue when the sun is high and, finally, a deep green in the twilight. In the early mornings, the fishing boats venture out and in the afternoon return with their catches, as squawking gulls follow alongside. Beside the house is a large, fresh-water pond ringed with wildlife— swans, ducks, herons, turtles, and the red-winged blackbirds whose raspy voices break the still air. A few months earlier, David, the assistant novice director, had told me the (true) story of a woman on retreat who had climbed onto an enormous rocky ledge on the beach by the house. Deep in meditation, she failed to notice the tide coming in. Finishing her prayer a few hours later, she turned around and found herself completely surrounded by the Atlantic. "What did she do?" I asked David.

"Well, it took another six hours before the tide went out," he said. "So she got in a *lot* of prayer!"

Things moved more rapidly after postulancy, as we settled down into novitiate life with the rest of the community. There were four second-year novices. George had been an air force captain and had worked with the Jesuit Volunteer Corps in Alaska. He had a wonderfully dry sense of humor. The day after entrance day, the novices went on a small picnic and George entertained me with one thing that I thought I would have to forego after entrance: Jesus jokes. Scandalous, yes, but hearing them from a novice helped me to relax a little. Tom, a gifted history teacher, was a shy person eager to make friends. Another Tom, older than me by ten years, had been a number of things—a soldier in Viet Nam, an interior designer, and a teacher. Michael, a former diocesan priest, completed the second-year class.

My own year included a recent graduate of the Jesuit-run College of the Holy Cross, named Bill and, somewhat more improbably, Emil, a forty-year-old Czech doctor. The seven of us would have been an unusual group in any situation other than a Jesuit novitiate. I soon realized that Jesuits attract very disparate types, which is a great part of their strength, but also the root of the challenges of living in community. I doubt there is any such thing as a "typical" Jesuit anymore than there is a "typical" Catholic. An older Jesuit told me that at one time you could ask three Jesuits from three different countries the same question and get the same answer. Now, he said with a laugh, you can be assured that you'd get at least three different answers—or four, depending on which Jesuits were asked.

In addition to the novice director and his assistant, there were a few other Jesuits living at the novitiate. John, from the New York province, was working on his doctor of ministry degree at Andover-Newton, a Protestant school of theology in the area. Dan taught at the Boston University School of Public Health, a Jesuit in a non-Jesuit institution. Joe, an older and experienced spiritual director, and a Jesuit brother named Bill completed the community. Bill was, in the parlance of the Society, the "minister" of the house, that is, he took care of the physical needs of the house. On entrance day, my mother, eager to make sense of all of this, asked Joe what he did.

"I'm a spiritual director."

"What's that?" asked my mom.

"Well, I listen to people talk about their prayer," said Joe.

"That's *it?*" she said.

"Yup," he laughed, delighted by such a direct question. "That's it!"

And after Bill explained his own tasks (pay the bills, call repairmen, and generally keep up the house), my mother started referring to herself as the minister of her house.

During the first weeks after postulancy, we "discerned" (a combination of prayer and decision making) our "ministry" for the fall. While we spent much of our time in the house in classes or in prayer, for ten or so hours a week we were expected to do some sort of work outside the house.

After visiting a few possible ministry placements, I was assigned, or more precisely was "missioned," to work in a hospital for the seriously ill. To the continuing consternation of the novice director, I persisted in referring to it as my "job," a reasonable enough mistake after six years at GE. We also received a monthly thirty-five-dollar stipend—called *personalia*—for "personal" things like toiletries, entertainment, stuff like that, which I likewise referred to as my "salary."

After our work was selected, we quickly settled into the Jesuit daily routine—our *ordo*. Morning prayer was at 7:15. I worried that I wouldn't know the prayers that everyone else knew or would forget the correct way to say the rosary. But I needn't have worried; as it turned out, morning prayer was far from rigid. We used the breviary once a week, but the rest of the time the novices were free to choose how they wanted to pray. Sometimes people handed out Xeroxed sheets of poems, songs, Scripture readings—anything they wanted to use for prayer. The Psalms were popular, too. We recited them antiphonally, that is, going back and forth from one side of the room to another, much in the way that monks chant when they gather for prayer. We also used a book called *Psalms Anew*, which featured "inclusive" language: *Yahweh* instead of *Lord*, *they* instead of *he*, *people* instead of *men*. Actually, until I entered the novitiate, I hadn't realized the Psalms were quite so violent. The sleepy morning voices of the novices would calmly intone verses about God killing our enemies and smashing their heads against the rocks. And then the refrain: "God is a loving God."

The novice director encouraged us to be creative in morning prayer. Thus, one morning in December, George, one of the *secundi*, proudly carried in a large ceramic bowl that he had filled with incense crystals. Great clouds of acrid smoke billowed from George's bowl, quickly filling the small chapel. Soon we were unable to breathe. The windows were quickly thrown open, and we found ourselves in a small, smoky, cold chapel. This proved not conducive to prayer, and George's incense bowl was never again seen at morning prayer.

On another morning, Bill played a tune for us on his saxophone. This, too, was less contemplative than the novice director intended.

After morning prayer, we would pad into the kitchen for a simple breakfast. Some of the novices, I noticed, had strange breakfast habits. Tom, for example, favored tuna fish salad on raisin bread, which made me gag each time I saw it. Since we were attempting to live simply at the novitiate, we cooked for ourselves. Given the number of people in the community, each person ended up cooking roughly three times a month. (Providing a good meal for your twelve housemates required spending the lion's share of the afternoon in the kitchen.) One novice, called a *manuductor* (from the Latin "to lead by the hand") coordinated who would set the tables before the meals and clean up afterwards. The *manuductor* also assigned the house jobs.

My house job was as shopper, which I found something of a challenge. Buying groceries for twelve people meant pushing three very full and very heavy shopping carts through the aisles at the Star Market which, since I was now living in Boston, was called the "Stah Mahket." I finally decided that the most efficient method was first to find out what I needed; next to park the carts in various aisles after I had filled them; and, finally, to corral them together—pushing one and dragging two—to the checkout counter. Inevitably, people in line asked for whom I was buying. One woman said, "Ooooh, let me guess! You're in a fraternity." (No, but a good guess.) "A fire station?" (Did I look like a fireman?) "It's a big party!" (Right, with ten heads of cauliflower.) After I told her the truth, she still appeared puzzled.

A few days before Christmas that year, I was missioned to buy ingredients for eggnog for the big novitiate party: ten dozen eggs and five gallons of cream. We were also low on butter, so I bought a dozen sticks. As I waited in the checkout line reading a magazine, the woman behind me tapped me on the shoulder. "Excuse me," she said quietly. "I hate to be nosy, but do you ever worry about your cholesterol?"

Following breakfast, at 8:00 sharp, we met for an hour-long "conference." The first year we covered the Jesuit *Constitutions*, written by St. Ignatius. Some of it was fascinating—seeing how Ignatius's spirituality was translated into a set of guidelines that have governed Jesuits for over 450 years. Some of the other parts, however, especially original directives that had later been superseded (but which were required reading nonetheless) were bizarre. There were, for example, rules governing what kind of nightclothes the scholastics would wear. Most of the conferences focused on discussions of Jesuit history and Jesuit spirituality. During the second year, we would review the vows—poverty, chastity, and obedience—which, though we had not yet "professed," were expected to follow.

Late mornings and afternoons were given over to working outside the house—our ministries or "apostolates." Mass was at 5:00 P.M. and dinner at 6:00. Some evenings we had community meetings, where we would discuss house "business"; sometimes a guest came to talk with the novices about his or her ministry: a sister working as a prison chaplain, a Jesuit Scripture scholar, a lay person running a homeless shelter.

Saturday mornings were wholly given over to *manualia*, the time when the novices were assigned to clean the house: cleaning toilets (their name was Legion, for they were many) scrubbing floors, mowing the lawn, washing the windows, or vacuuming and polishing everything in the very large novitiate. Sometimes George, *manuductor* for my first year, would assign more bothersome jobs, like returning the empty soda (or "tonic" as they say in Boston) cans to the store. Since we were thirteen men and with a fridge always full of soda, our empties consisted of a dozen noisome trash bags filled with the sticky, empty cans. I thought *manualia* was suitably ascetic for Jesuits, but was somewhat annoyed after it emerged that the "fathers" were not responsible for any of the weekend *manualia*. This, I was told when I broached the subject, was simply the way it was done. But it was maddening when, for example, I vacuumed the living room while some of the fathers read the morning papers. When the vacuum approached, they would lift their feet to allow the novice to clean around them.

In the midst of all this activity, we prayed. At least one hour of contemplative prayer, daily Mass, and the *examen* at night. The *examen* is a short prayer devised by St. Ignatius in which you try to see how God was active during your day. First, you give thanks to God for all of the graces you had received during the day. Anything you were grateful for: the sight of sunlight on the pavement; the taste of an orange; a joke shared with someone; or maybe a particularly rewarding moment at work (or getting an easy job for *manualia*). Second, you ask for the grace to see where God had been with you during the day.

Next you review the entire day. Where you had accepted God's grace—in other words, where you had followed what you thought God might want you to do, and where you hadn't. This part of the *examen* is almost like rewinding the day and playing it back, like a movie. Finally, you ask God for forgiveness of your sins and for the grace to do better the next day.

The whole prayer might last only fifteen minutes, the bulk of it taken up with the review of the day. (Some Jesuits also pray the *examen* at noon.) But despite its length, the *examen* is an extremely helpful method of prayer. In fact, St. Ignatius used to say that if there is only time for one private prayer a day, it should be given over to the *examen*, so much did he value it. It's easy to see why: it's a grace in itself to be able to see where God has been active in your day, what gifts you've received from God, and where you consistently need God's help. The *examen* helps to get your spiritual house in order, quickly.

There was also regular weekly spiritual direction, along the lines of what happened during my first retreat. Initially, I was daunted by the idea of praying every day and felt the urge to "produce," that is, to get results. And this prompted some worries: What if my prayer wasn't as good as it was on retreat? What if I found I *couldn't* pray and the retreat was a fluke? What if, as a result, I discovered I was in the wrong place? After all, most of the novices had considerably more experience in prayer and retreats than I did.

Fortunately, my spiritual director, David Donovan, was both well trained in the art of direction and enormously patient, and had had his share of, well, novices when it came to prayer. Prayer, he liked to say, is a "long, loving look at the real," another way of expressing the Jesuit ideal of finding God in all

things—in your work, in your community, in your joys and sor-
rows. The stuff of prayer and reflection was, David explained,
the stuff of your life. Starting out from that assumption made
prayer seem more accessible for me, and more natural.

IT WAS A GOOD life. Certainly more human than the one at GE,
which was already beginning to seem far away. Still, I had quite
a few difficulties that year. First, my parents were still separated; my mom still called very frequently, and I began to feel
that I had somehow "abandoned" my family, that I was selfish
for wanting to be a Jesuit. But my mother and sister visited the
novitiate often during the first year, which served to remove
some of the mystery of Jesuit life for them. They might not
have completely understood the Society of Jesus at first (nor
did I, for that matter), but they certainly liked the Jesuits that
they knew. Other friends came to stay as well. Bruce said it was
his favorite bed & breakfast.

Every Sunday night the novices gathered in the living room
for "faith sharing," where we talked about our prayer over the
past week. At first, listening to the other novices talk about the
rich experiences they found in prayer provoked envy. If I
wanted to measure up to the other novices, I thought, I have to
work more diligently at prayer. Pretty much the type of thinking I engaged in at Wharton and on the job. Competing and
comparing myself with others, even in prayer.

But I could engage in this kind of thinking for only a short
while before realizing its futility. God is the one who enables
prayer, not the person praying. After hearing this from David
about fifty times, I relaxed and started to enjoy seeing how
God worked in the lives of the other novices—coming to one
person through music, to another through reading, to another
through a Jesuit or their families or an experience in ministry.
God, as I would hear more than a few times, meets people
where they are.

The novitiate also opened a new chapter of reading for me.
I could continue the religious education that stopped so many
years ago in C.C.D.

Despite all my prayers to St. Jude, I had always found it difficult to appreciate devotion to saints. It seemed faintly superstitious. All that stuff about St. Anthony finding lost things. ("St. Anthony, St. Anthony, please come around. Something is lost and cannot be found.") Saint Joseph helping you sell a house. (Burying a statue of St. Joseph in your backyard struck me as quite the *opposite* of a "devotion.") What's the use if you have Jesus? I thought. But those questions were laid to rest when I began to read the lives of the saints that filled the wooden shelves of the novitiate library.

After reading just a few biographies, I finally recognized the saints for who they were: companions, and an effective way of understanding how God works in different times, different circumstances, and different lives. I first picked up the frank autobiography of St. Thérèse of Lisieux called *Story of a Soul*. Thérèse has often been portrayed in saccharine hagiography as a passive and docile child: the Little Flower. But in her autobiography, she comes alive as an intelligent young woman with a implacable faith in God, and—better yet—a sense of humor. Her wonderful story led me to hunt down others in the library: St. Stanislaus Kostka, a young Jesuit saint who, despite the protests of his family, walked 450 miles to the novitiate; St. Aloysius Gonzaga, a Jesuit scholastic who cared for plague victims in Rome before himself succumbing to sickness and exhaustion. The great North American Jesuit martyrs like St. Isaac Jogues and St. Jean de Brébeuf, who worked among the Huron Indians in the seventeenth century. And contemporary saints like Dorothy Day, Archbishop Oscar Romero, Pope John XXIII and, of course, Thomas Merton. I found a superlative biography of Merton called *The Seven Mountains of Thomas Merton*, by Michael Mott, that had appeared just that year, which told me much more about Merton's turbulent life. The lives of the saints opened a whole world that had been closed to me, a world that I ignored, just as Charles Ryder had described it in *Brideshead Revisited*. I read that novel once again, too, and was surprised to discover how much, at its heart, it is a book about faith.

The novices were also expected that fall to read a number of biographies of St. Ignatius, plus his own autobiography, as a way of coming to know the Jesuit history and "charism," or spirit, of the order. Not surprisingly, I was almost completely unfamiliar with the story of St. Ignatius.

Iñigo of Loyola was born in 1491 in the Basque country of Northern Spain. As a boy he served as a page in the court of a local nobleman and later distinguished himself as a valiant soldier. He was, as he describes in his autobiography, "a man given over to the vanities of the world," particularly concerning his physical appearance. He seems also to have been a ladies' man, or at least that's how he fancied himself. He was definitely a rake. It was rumored that he fathered an illegitimate child.

During a battle in Pamplona, at the beginning of his soldiering career, Iñigo's leg was struck by a cannonball. He was carried out of battle on a litter and brought to a cousin's home to recuperate. The bone in his leg was set poorly and Iñigo, who wanted his leg to look smart in his courtier's tights, submitted to a series of gruesome and painful operations. But the leg never healed properly, and he was left with a lifelong limp.

With so much time on his sickbed, Iñigo asked a relative for some books. Unfortunately, all she had to offer was pious reading, which he took grudgingly. To his surprise, Iñigo found himself attracted to the lives of the saints, and found himself thinking, "If St. Francis or St. Dominic could do such and such, maybe I could do great things." He also noticed that, after thinking about doing things for God, he was left with a feeling of peace—what he termed "consolation." On the other hand, after thinking about succeeding as a soldier or impressing a particular woman, though initially filled with great enthusiasm, later he would be left feeling "dry." Slowly, he recognized these feelings of dryness and consolation as ways that God was leading him to follow the right path.

Iñigo decided that, after he recovered, he would become a pilgrim and tramp to the Holy Land and see what he might do there in God's service. Before leaving, he made a pilgrimage to a famous monastery in Spain, in Montserrat, where he laid aside his knightly armor and put on the homespun garb of a pilgrim. From Montserrat, Iñigo journeyed to a small town called Manresa, where he lived the life of a poor pilgrim, fasting continually, and begging for alms. During his time in Manresa, he experienced a deep sense of union with God, making him certain that he was being called to follow God more closely. After spending several months in seclusion and experiencing prayer that grew ever more profound, Iñigo commenced his journey to Jerusalem.

After a series of mishaps in Jerusalem and elsewhere, he realized that to accomplish anything of value in the Church at the time, he would need more education, and perhaps even have to become a priest. So the former soldier vowed to recommence his education, an arduous process that took him to the university cities of Alcalá, Salamanca and, finally, Paris. This also meant that, since he had little knowledge of Latin, he would have to sit in class—at age thirty—with small boys learning their Latin lessons.

While studying in Paris, Iñigo attracted a good deal of attention as a result of his ascetical penchant for dressing in the poorest clothes, begging for alms, helping the poor, and assisting other students in prayer. In Paris he also completed what would later become known as his *Spiritual Exercises*, a series of meditations on God's love and the life of Jesus designed to help people draw closer to God. Iñigo also led his new roommate, Francisco Javier, through these exercises. Later he would become better known, of course, as St. Francis Xavier, one of the Church's great missionaries. Iñigo, at this time, changed his own name, to the more Latin-sounding Ignatius.

Gradually, Ignatius gathered around him a tight-knit group of six men, who decided they would work together in the service of God. But to do what? Ultimately, they decided to present themselves directly to the pope, who would be better able to discern a direction for the group. Eventually, the men decided to form the Company of Jesus, or *Societas* in Latin, for the purpose of, among other things, "helping souls." At first, Ignatius had a tough time winning acceptance for his Society. For one thing, some in the church hierarchy were disturbed that he was not founding a more traditional monastic order, with an emphasis on common prayer and a stricter community life. But Ignatius's men (who were derisively called "Jesuits" by their opponents) wanted to be out in the world. Ignatius, ever resourceful, shrewdly enlisted the help of powerful churchmen to speak on the Society's behalf.

It was from these humble efforts that the Society of Jesus began. After they settled in Rome and received papal approval for their new order, Ignatius began the arduous task of writing the Jesuits' constitutions and laying out plans for their work. Ignatius proved both ambitious and persistent. At the same time, he was flexible and ready to do God's will. He fought for the Society whenever a church official raised another objection about his new order. Yet he used to say that if the pope ordered the Jesuits to disband, he would need only fifteen minutes in prayer to compose himself and be on his way.

Saint Ignatius was presented to the novices as the model Jesuit: intelligent, prayerful, and *disponible*—available, readily disposed to do God's will. He was ambitious to do great things for God, *Ad majorem Dei Gloriam*, for the greater glory of God. Another way of expressing this was the Jesuit tradition of the *magis*—the best, the highest, the most for God. Indeed, it has often been noted how fortunate it was for the Catholic Church that Ignatius transformed his worldly ambitions into ambitions for the Church. His courtier's charm, his soldier's tenacity, and his stalwart temperament all combined to make him a formidable first superior of the Jesuits. While he professed complete obedience to the Church, he never hesitated to push and push and push until he received the final "no." He was not a man to be trifled with and neither were the first Jesuits.

Ignatius was tough. Perhaps there was less of a difference between the Society of Jesus and the corporate world than I had first thought. Of course, the goals were different—devotion to money versus devotion to God—but there was a tenacity in Ignatius that made me think he might have done pretty well at

GE. For a mystic, Ignatius was also eminently practical. At one point, one of his charges wrote him from Spain and complained that by asking for money from a benefactor he was "bending the knee to Baal," in other words, acting in a too-worldly fashion instead of relying on divine providence. Ignatius responded, didn't Joseph use his position at Pharaoh's court to help his brothers? Didn't St. Paul appeal to his Roman citizenship to escape his enemies? You are being, said Ignatius, "overly spiritual." Of course, this practical Ignatius was the same person who frequently was unable to continue celebrating a Mass because he was overcome with "the gift of tears." But he knew that he lived in a real, tangible, human world. It was this example of Ignatius—a practical mystic—that animated his Jesuits to be "contemplatives in action" working for the *magis*, God's greater glory.

THE *MAGIS*, by the way, was part of a whole new language to learn—the language of "religious" and of the Society of Jesus. Even the term "religious," which refers to a member of a religious order, was a new one for me.

Until just a few decades ago, most Jesuit formation was conducted in Latin, even during recreation and meals. As a result, while Jesuit life today is conducted in the vernacular, Latin lives on in the often arcane lingo of the Society of Jesus. First-year novices are *primi* (which made me think of premature babies) and second-year novices, *secundi*. Besides *manualia*, Jesuits used to do a lot of *laborandum*, which was heavier work outdoors. An *informatio* is an evaluation that other Jesuits are asked to complete when someone moves on to the next stage in formation. There were "formed" Jesuits and Jesuits "in formation," which made those of us in training sound like lumps of clay.

The daily order in most novitiates was still referred to as the *ordo*. Those about to be ordained are *ordinandi;* those taking vows, *vovendi*. The comprehensive exam taken at the end of philosophy studies is the *De Universa* or *De U*, for short. (Literally "Of all things.")

Saint Ignatius was fond of the concept, often mentioned in the novitiate, of *agere contra*. This meant that if you felt a strong disinclination or repugnance in doing something, you should work against it—not merely for the sake of doing so, but to rid yourself of something that might keep you from being freer and more "available." As one example, I dreaded being asked to work in a hospital, so one day my novice director asked me if I wanted to think about *agere contra*. I did, and realized Ignatius was right. Working in that setting helped to free me of all sort of misconceptions about hospitals and the sick.

Each provincial was assisted by the province *socius*. Each community had a superior, or if it was a large community, a "rector," who was appointed by the superior general in Rome. Most communities had someone in charge of guest rooms, the "guestmaster." Some novitiates had a "beadle," in charge of house assignments. ("The *beetle?*" I asked when I first heard about this.) Sometimes larger communities would have an *admonitor* to keep an eye on the superior.

To ice the cake, the New England Province Catalog (excuse me, the *Catalogus Provinciae Novae Angliae*) was, until two years after I entered, an impenetrable thicket of Latin. The catalog contained the locations and jobs of all the New England Province Jesuits. On the page for the novitiate *(Domus Probationis Arrupe House)*, the novice director was listed as:

> *P. Gerald J. Calhoun—Sup. NN. a die 31 jul. 1985,*
> *Mag. nov., Exam. candid., Conf. dom. et nov.*

Which meant, Fr. *(Pater)* Calhoun, had been superior of our *(NN: nostri)* novitiate since July 31, 1985. His jobs included those of the novice director *(Magister novitii)* and as confessor for the house *(dom.)* and the novices. He also examined the candidates for the Society.

All Jesuits in the province were grouped together in the back of the *Index Alphabeticus Sociorum Ineunte Anno 1988*. This long alphabetical index included notations indicating your

Jesuit superior as well as your birth date, your date of entrance, the date of your final vows and, if you were a priest, the date of your ordination. The next year, I flipped to the back of the book and saw my name under *Nostri in formatione*, under *Anno 1988 Ingressi:* I felt like an official Jesuit. There were also lists of *Vita functii* (Jesuits who had died during the past year), *Elenchus dismissorum* (those who had left), and *Expect. dest.* (those waiting for a new assignment).

I also learned from the province catalog that every Jesuit in the Society had a ministry, *every* one. Those too ill for "active" ministry were still listed as *Cur. val.*, short for *curat valitudenem*, "Caring for his health." The very sick, perhaps those who were awaiting death in the infirmary, were listed as *Orat pro Eccles. et Soc:* "Praying for the Church and the Society." I liked this idea. One older Jesuit told me that over the bed of one of the more notorious smokers in the philosophate, some of his Jesuit brothers had posted a sign saying *Fumat pro Eccles. et Soc.* ("Smoking for the Church and the Society"). Other Jesuits joked about having entries like *Bib. Whisk., Lec. Temp., Vid. Tel.* ("Drinks whiskey, reads the *Times*, watches television").

But there was more than just the Jesuit lingo to be mastered. There was two thousand years of unfamiliar Catholic terminology: corporals, chasubles, stoles, lectionaries, sacramentaries, albs, patens, censers, and purificators. These were things. Vicars, deacons, curates, sacristans, and acolytes, on the other hand, were people.

And—my God—the religious orders! The Benedictines, the Dominicans, the Franciscans. The Passionists, Redemptorists, Vincentians, Assumptionists, Sulpicians, Servites, Salesians. The Comboni Fathers, the Consolata Fathers, the Paulist Fathers, the Piarist Fathers, the Marist Fathers. The Oblates of Mary, the Franciscan Missionaries of Mary, the Sisters of the Immaculate Heart of Mary. The Sisters of Our Lady of Lourdes, of Notre Dame de Namur, of the Sacred Heart, of Saint Joseph. The Sisters of Charity *and* the Daughters of Charity. The Little Sisters of Jesus, the Little Sisters of Jesus and Mary,

and the Little Sisters of the Poor. The Poor Clares. The Grey
Nuns. The Camaldolese. The Dimesse Sisters. And the Pre-
monstratensians. (I could hardly even *pronounce* that last one.)
One day I took a message from a nun who said she was
calling from Senegal. A few hours later, David, the assistant
novice director, held out my phone message and asked, "What
does this say?"

"Oh," I said, "who do you know in Senegal?"

"No one!" David said, "are you sure she said *Senegal?*"

"Yeah, I think so."

David started laughing. "No, she's from the *Cenacle!*" He
could barely catch his breath. "Not Senegal!"

"Oh, yeah? What's the Cenacle?"

He caught his breath. "It's a religious order. It's named
after the Upper Room."

"Oh," I said. Of course, I hadn't the vaguest idea what the
Upper Room was. (It's where the Last Supper was held.)

The novitiate also signaled the beginning of my informal
education of Jesuit history: stories from older Jesuits. Such
tales typically began, "When *I* was a novice . . ." a sort of a
variation on the "When *I* was your age . . ." stories that children hear from their parents. There were plenty of horror stories from decades past that frankly astonished me, making our
own novitiate seem almost shockingly lax. Seeing your family
only on "visiting" days, not being able to attend a parent's
funeral; these were commonplace. One Jesuit told me that he
was happy his mother had died after he had taken first vows.
Had she died *before* he had taken vows, he would have been
forbidden to go to the funeral. Novices then were also forbidden during "recreation" from walking with just one other
novice. Groups of three were the way to prevent "particular
friendships." *Numquam duo, semper tres* ("Never two, always
three"). For the most part, though, the older fathers treated
these reminiscences with an equal mixture of nostalgia and
healthy criticism.

There had been rules for everything, and even a "Customs
Book" for American Jesuits, which detailed such things as what

Jesuits wore, what the tombstones were to look like, and the precise types of food to be served on different liturgical feasts like Christmas, Easter, and feast days of Jesuit saints. (Oysters, for some reason, seemed to be a big deal.)

Though many of these customs have been abandoned, younger Jesuits still find themselves living with men who were "formed" under this old system. Some fathers who remember the time when a novice wouldn't even speak to a father may find it surprising when a young Jesuit makes a sarcastic remark at the dinner table. In my novitiate community, the ages ranged from twenty-three to seventy. During philosophy studies, I lived with a man who was eighty-five (and who, I should add, put in a full day's work). Indeed, the Society of Jesus is one of the last places in this country where you still live with your brothers, fathers, and grandfathers.

Part III

Late Have I Loved You

Late have I loved you,
O Beauty so ancient and so new;
late have I loved you! . . .
You did call and cry to me and
break open my deafness;
and you did send forth your light
and shine upon me and chase away my blindness;
you did breathe fragrance upon me,
and I drew in my breath and now long for you;
I tasted you and now hunger and thirst for you;
you touched me and I have burned for your peace.

St. Augustine, *Confessions*

7.

Religious by Nature

*If a person leaves his dreamy conceptions aside, and focuses on
his naked poverty, when the masks fall and the core of his
being is revealed, it soon becomes obvious that he is religious
by nature. In the midst of his existence there unfolds the bond
(re-ligio) which ties him to the infinitely transcendent
mystery of God, the insatiable interest in the absolute that
captivates him and underlines his poverty.*

Johannes Metz, *Poverty of Spirit*

Having geared myself to a finance job in a comfortable
office (preferably one with a window), I found my fall
ministry exceedingly difficult. Youville Hospital in Cambridge,
a place for the seriously ill and dying, was an hour's ride on the
subway (the "T" in Boston) from the novitiate. It was founded
by the Grey Nuns, a Canadian order of sisters with a long tradition of hospital ministry with people of all faiths. The patients
at Youville suffered from multiple sclerosis, brain damage, cancer, AIDS, and other illnesses; many were comatose.

I was assigned to work with the pastoral care staff, which
comprised three former sisters, two Franciscan priests, and one
married layman. It was a wonderful group of kind and knowl-
edgeable people, and I had the opportunity to "reflect" with the
layman on the staff, named Ernie, every week. Most of the time
I talked to Ernie about how difficult it was for me just to *be* in
a hospital. And while the psychological difficulties of being
around death and suffering and illness were challenging, it was

the more mundane things—the smells, sights, and sounds—
that really got to me. Especially the smells.

At first I was intent on "performing," on *doing* something,
in an environment where it quickly became apparent that I
could, in fact, do very little. My job was to visit the patients and
listen to them talk about . . . whatever. Or, if they were unable
to talk, just to sit with them. Never had I felt so awkward and
out of place in my life. And so useless. But this, Ernie kept
reminding me, was part of the experience—not so much feeling awkward as realizing there was not a whole lot I could do
except be there. It did wonders for one's humility.

It was an utterly new type of work, the opposite of what I
had done at GE. There was little emphasis on "producing."
There were no deadlines. It wasn't competitive. That didn't
mean that the people with whom I worked on the pastoral care
team weren't professionals. They simply weren't interested in
whether you were a high pot or a low pot, a 1, 2, or 3, or
whether or not you had made your monthly numbers. They
were more interested in finding God in their work.

The patients were a remarkable mix of people, all of
whom, of course, had suffered and were struggling to live with
their illnesses. One woman, Rita, had been at Youville for
twenty years. Remember, Ernie told me, when you walk into
the hospital rooms of many of the patients, you're walking into
their homes. And, indeed, Rita's hospital room looked like anyone else's bedroom, with pillows and candles on a shelf by her
bed and postcards and photos of long-dead family members
taped to the wall. The difference, of course, was that there were
three other hospital beds in Rita's room, one of which was
occupied by a comatose woman. A few weeks before Christmas, Rita asked me to retrieve a dusty box of ornaments that
she stored in her closet, so we could decorate her room for the
holidays. The decorations were taped up in the same place she
had put them for the past twenty years. There were even tiny
pencil marks on the wall to indicate where to hang the cardboard Christmas tree, the manger scene, and the angel. Rita had
two older brothers in the Jesuits and a sister who was a nun, so

we had plenty to talk about. "The Jesuits," she declared one day, "are the best order."

Another patient, named Gladys, was a frail, elderly woman dying of cancer. Tubes and wires snaked out from under her bedcovers and coiled their way across the floor to a thicket of monitors and bags. She had been a teacher in a small Massachusetts town and, after her retirement, had lived with her single sister in the house in which they had been born. Gladys had never married but, at one time, had a sweetheart in the navy. Sometimes she confused me with her sweetheart and told me how handsome I looked in my uniform and how happy she was that I had made it home from sea.

Gene was a twenty-five-year-old man who had severe brain damage as a result of a motorcycle accident when he was fifteen. Gene had the use of only one arm, which he used to direct his crumpled fingers to big block letters printed on a small tray connected to his wheelchair. This was how he communicated.

At first I avoided Gene because he had a habit of drooling, which I found hard to watch. But I soon got used to this and ended up spending a great deal of my time with him. We visited almost every day, and I enjoyed the conversations he spelled out on his board. Gene was excellent company and had a surprisingly dry sense of humor. He especially liked to make fun of the nurses. When he saw me walking down the hall, he would grin at me with half-closed eyes and toss his head back. That was the signal that he was ready for a conversation.

Most of the patients at Youville had some particular trait that initially repulsed me, but once I got over the shock of their physical situations, I was more able to enjoy them for who they were. They stopped being simply "patients" and, instead, became individuals, friends. And despite Ernie telling me how important it was to just be with them, I was happiest when I could actually "do" something for them, like read to them, feed them, help them get dressed, or wheel them to the chapel for daily Mass.

But sometimes, when the patients on my floor weren't awake, or if they were busy with physical therapy, there wasn't much to do and I grew bored. To kill time, I would hang out in the pastoral care office flipping through old magazines and books, wander around the hospital, and even stand on the outdoor porch, lean on the railing, and look at the trees in Cambridge turning scarlet and orange. But soon I realized that whether or not I was obsessed with "doing something," this was a waste of time. I finally decided that when there was nothing else to do, I could at least sit by the beds of the comatose patients and pray for them.

Some days were especially difficult, and I felt that I wasn't at all cut out for hospital ministry. It was especially hard breaking the ice with new patients or talking with patients who were depressed. And I could hardly blame them. Who wants to be cheerful in a hospital? And who would want to talk about their problems to someone they had never met? I could imagine wanting to be alone myself. Not surprisingly, there were many patients at Youville who were angry and depressed about being there. Some would just sit silently in their wheelchairs or lie in their beds weeping in a tangle of sheets.

On Friday afternoons we gathered together a "prayer group," during which everyone discussed the gospel reading for the coming Sunday. Sometimes one of the pastoral care members would open the afternoon with a song. I was amazed by the depth of patients' faith life—not by how simple or childlike their faith was, but by how well developed it was. Much more so than mine.

During one session, the reading focused on the meaning of the cross. Doris, with multiple sclerosis, said that the cross reminded her of her wheelchair. Many people, she said, look at their wheelchairs (most of the people in the room were in one) as burdens—reminders of your weakness—things that slow you down. I think that's true, she said, but there's more.

"For me," she said, "it helps me do everything—get around, see people, be myself. Without my wheelchair, my life would be so dull."

I was amazed by her insight. It was completely true and—like the truth that Jesus revealed in the Gospels—utterly surprising. Better than any description of the cross I had heard. And better than anything I could have come up with in a thousand years of reflection.

After a day's work at the hospital, it was good to walk through Harvard Square in the cool fall afternoons, ride the "T" over the Charles River, and think. I couldn't believe how much my life had changed in just a few months. Working in the hospital with very ill people, confronting death and suffering every day, going to Mass seven days a week. I'd walk in the fading afternoon sunlight from the "T," by the housing projects, past the Dominican- and Puerto Rican-owned record stores, laundromats, and *bodegas*, past the immense parish church and into our warm house, where I'd climb the stairs to the quiet chapel for Mass.

Ernie and I became friends and, one night, I invited his family to the novitiate for dinner. He came along with his wife and his eleven-year-old son, Gabriel, to Arrupe House. Gabriel was quite taken with the novitiate and marveled at the fact that one of our refrigerators was stocked with nothing but soda. This was actually something of a contentious issue in the novitiate. There were some (myself included) who thought that having ten different types of sodas represented something less than a simple lifestyle. The majority, however (including the novice director, who was the only majority that counted in this instance), countered that it wasn't surprising we drank so much soda with thirteen people in the house. In any event, Gabriel's eyes widened when he opened the fridge, "Wow!" he said. "Look at all these *sodas!* I want to live here!"

"Well," I said as we stood in front of the fridge, "if you have to live here, you have to be poor and not have any money." Gabriel silently considered the trade-off.

"That's okay," he said. "I don't have any money anyway!"

"And you can't have any girlfriends and you have to listen to whatever the novice director says."

"I don't have any girlfriends anyway," he said. "and I have to listen to my parents anyway." He paused for a moment of reflection. "I might as well join! I can have free sodas!"

Actually, we seemed to have plenty of everything. I was, therefore, occasionally disappointed that we didn't seem to live what—at the time—I considered to be "real" poverty. In addition to the unlimited sodas and snacks (a luxury that most middle-class people don't have—let alone the poor), we ate well and lived in a comfortable house. But I had to admit that this was probably not too far from what Ignatius intended. "The manner of living is ordinary," he wrote in the *Constitutions*, in other words, like the people around us. And, for the most part, we were living according to his dictum. Still, it bothered some of the other novices as well, whose idea of Jesuit poverty was sometimes different from the way it played out in Jesuit life.

But I didn't have many other complaints about the novitiate. I was delighted to be there and happy to be out of the corporate world. And, as an added benefit, I wasn't having nearly as many stomach problems. ("How do your intestines like the novitiate?" asked a friend a few months after I entered.)

The novitiate was a good time to take stock. Arrupe House was a place to step back and, most of all, to reflect. A perfect word: *reflect*. I could be calm, like a still pond, and reflect what had happened to me in the past—my experiences with my family, my friends, my time at work, my desires, loves, frustrations—and bring it before God in prayer.

I also realized, slowly at first, that the Society of Jesus was not perfect. There were plenty of very holy Jesuits, but there were also ones with whom I probably wouldn't have chosen to live outside the Society. And, like any human organization, the Jesuits had their problems. I was surprised by this but, in retrospect, I shouldn't have been. Thomas Merton even talked about it in *The Seven Storey Mountain,* when he wrote:

> The first and most elementary test of one's call to the religious life—whether as a Jesuit, Franciscan, Cistercian or Carthusian—is the willingness to accept life in a community in which everybody is more or less imperfect.

Including oneself of course. My reactions about poverty, for example, sprung not only from reflecting on some real problems in the Society but also from my own tendency to judge based on a few quick impressions.

Thomas Merton discusses such realizations in greater detail in *The Sign of Jonas*, written during his first years in the monastery, when some of the "first fervor"—his romanticism about religious life—wears off, while his faith continues to deepen. He complains constantly about his superiors (*especially* his superiors), the work, the weather, the food, the bugs (at least we had screens at Arrupe House), and religious life in general. Reading his book in the novitiate helped me bridge the gap between starry-eyed idealism and something approaching realism.

I found, for example, while our novice director was a compassionate man, a good Jesuit, and an excellent spiritual director, he could be something of a drill sergeant when it came to matters of the house. When we had *manualia*, the window shades had to be pulled down to a precise level (halfway) and the kitchen needed to be cleaned a particular way. The kitchen cabinet doors always had to be closed, the table set a certain way, and newspapers never to be brought into the dining room. Part of this was necessary to keep order in a large community, and it did make the house a more pleasant place to live—but it still annoyed me.

What's more, since I was forever forgetting things and, moreover, forgetting that I was no longer living in my own apartment, some of my old habits bugged the novice director to no end. When I was working in Stamford, I found that the best way to keep track of my car keys was to put them in my coat pocket. After a few years, I did this without thinking. But doing the same thing at the novitiate meant that the keys to the community cars would frequently disappear into my coat pockets. One day I went to Youville with the keys and came home to find that a novice had signed out that car for the day. He was rightly furious at my forgetfulness.

The care of car keys wasn't the only contentious issue between myself and the novice director. I sometimes found that my innate corporate mentality often ran up against the Jesuit "way of proceeding."

In October, for example, the novice director asked me to "facilitate" a community meeting regarding the house chapel. Since the novitiate was still relatively new, our chapel hadn't yet been decorated. Jerry suggested a few questions for the discussion. Should we have stained glass windows? More decorations for the walls? A music system for playing tapes?

Having chaired numerous meetings at GE, I had no problem running this one. We discussed the questions one by one. It took us less than an hour to come to clear conclusions about the way the chapel should look. Of course, I knew that the novice director retained the final say about the chapel but, surprisingly, he said little during the meeting. That such a large group could have decided these things in such a short period of time seemed quite an accomplishment. Maybe I'd get some brownie points for my efficiency.

The next day the novice director asked to see me. No doubt to congratulate me for the meeting. He asked me if I thought the meeting had gone well.

That's a strange way of congratulating me, I thought.

I said that I thought it had.

"Well, I didn't," he said. "You know, a few people didn't get the chance to talk about how they felt."

Huh?

"Not everyone was heard from, Jim. There were some people who didn't say anything last night."

Wasn't that their problem? I wondered.

Apparently not.

"You know," he explained, "it wasn't as important that we *decide* something in the meeting as it was that we discussed it and discovered one another's views."

"But wasn't the point actually to decide something?"

"Not necessarily," he said.

I could see his point—the inherent value of discussion in a community meeting. But, unfortunately, this sometimes meant that actual decisions were a long way off. Indeed, the ideas decided upon at that meeting never were put into action. In the end, the novice director did decide what should be done with the chapel, which ended up being pretty much the opposite of the recommendations from the meeting. And while I recognized the value of discussion, I thought action was important, too. I wondered if the novitiate could learn something from corporate America.

Being a novice also involved some unavoidable regression, and I sometimes felt that I was back in adolescence. Not to say that I was *always* treated like a teenager, but having to ask permission for things that many adults took for granted proved something of a shock. Using a community car, traveling more than thirty-five miles away, asking for money for a new pair of shoes. Add to that being told how to perform any number of tasks—clean the kitchen, lower the blinds, set the table—and it engendered what we novices called "infantilization," especially after having lived on our own. Tom, for example, had run a successful business. George had lived in various air force bases across the world and had worked with the Jesuit Volunteer Corps, an organization of young lay persons, in Alaska for a year. Michael had run numerous parishes as a diocesan priest. None of us were children, yet we sometimes felt that we were being treated like that. It was something to get used to and, in the time-honored tradition of religious novices everywhere, to complain about. Much of this, of course, fell under the heading of "obedience," but even if intellectually and spiritually I understood the purpose, it bothered my oversized ego not to be in control.

Though this did not mean I had no say about my life (in fact, I think I had more say in the Jesuits than I ever did in GE), and was more carefully listened to, obedience represented a clear change in my life. It was the same with poverty. While I wasn't going hungry, there was a marked difference in how I lived. On thirty-five dollars a month, there is only so much you can do, so many movies, so many books, and so many restaurants you can enjoy.

When the cold weather hit Boston, I went to the house "minister," the Jesuit brother who handled the cash. I needed to buy a hat. How much did I need? he asked. Well, I didn't have a credit card, so I figured I could just take a wad of money to the store, buy a hat, and return the change.

"Oh, give me about thirty dollars," I said. Instead, after regarding me for a second, he then handed me a five-dollar bill and told me to take the rest from my budget. Needless to say, this sort of limitation forced me to be more frugal than I would have been with thirty dollars in my pocket. All I could find was a ten-dollar wool beret in Cambridge. "Any change?" he asked when I returned.

I also, right off the bat, decided to cancel my many credit cards. I certainly wasn't going to charge things anymore. (How would I pay for them anyway? At thirty-five dollars a month, I couldn't even afford the annual service fees.) Actually, I was delighted to get rid of them and further simplify my life. So one morning after conference, I called the American Express people and instructed them to cancel my account. The customer service rep asked for my card number, and I could hear him punching up my account on his computer.

"Oh, Mr. Martin," he said, "you've been a *very* good customer. Why are you canceling your card?"

Great. The last thing I wanted to do was explain religious life to American Express.

"Um, I've joined a religious order?" I said tentatively. "And I don't have much money. We, uh, take a vow of poverty and . . . "

"A religious order? Which one?" he asked.

"The Jesuits."

"No kidding," he said. "My spiritual director is a Jesuit!"

He is?

"Have you ever been to Campion Center?" he asked.

"Uh, yeah."

"Well, I go there all the *time* for retreats! I love the Jesuits! You're calling from Boston, aren't you? So that means you're in the New England Province, right? Listen, I'll tell you what. I know about your vow of poverty and all that, so I'll just set your account aside, and if you ever want to reactivate it, you just give us a call, okay? And say a prayer for me."

"Sure. Thanks!" I said. What service.

Another challenge came with the novitiate's emphasis on introspection, which could sometimes lead to the rather skewed view of yourself as the center of the universe. It was quite the opposite of life at GE, where the individual seemed to matter little. Of course, this was a religious order, where reflection and prayer were both necessary and valuable, but I began to wonder if there was such a thing as too much reflection. (It was at that point that I realized I would have made a lousy monk.) We had weekly one-on-one spiritual direction to discuss our prayer, weekly meetings with our work supervisor, weekly community "faith sharing" to discuss our prayer and our work, monthly meetings with the novice director and, finally, weekly "reflections" to discuss what we learned in conference. Since we worked outside of the house ten to fifteen hours a week, most of our lives revolved around life in the novitiate which, in turn, revolved around the novices.

On the other hand, one could just as easily develop a low opinion of oneself. The same introspection engendered a greater awareness of your faults and weaknesses. Some of this was salutary—an honest understanding of your own weaknesses could lead to spiritual growth and to a deeper humility. I realized, for example, that I was overly concerned with whether I was making a good impression. Also known in the spiritual life as pride.

But sometimes the hothouse environment of the novitiate could result in a *very* low opinion of oneself. Peccadillos could sometimes be magnified into major spiritual problems. Was I too "controlling" because I wanted to run meetings? Was I "passive-aggressive" because I kept leaving the cabinet doors open? Perhaps I was controlling *and* passive-aggressive! On the other hand, maybe I was simply efficient in one case and forgetful in another. In the end, the novitiate required the novices to be prayerful and self-aware, and to strike an artful balance between mindless activity and narcissistic navel-gazing.

EVENTUALLY, Thanksgiving rolled around. For some of us novices, it was the first time away from our families at Thanksgiving, and I thought I would miss being home. I did but, as it turned out, I also enjoyed staying in Boston. Unlike any other Thanksgiving in the past, I worked, spending the day at Youville Hospital visiting the patients. Very few of the hospital staff were around, so it was an empty, still place.

For a few patients, I was their only visitor on Thanksgiving Day, since their relatives and old friends either had died or no longer visited them. I made my way around to the people I knew, and sat for a long while with Gladys. We watched the Macy's Thanksgiving Day Parade in New York. "Would you look at that," she would say as a particularly colorful balloon passed. Gladys fell asleep for a few minutes and then woke up and told me how happy she was that I had come home from the navy to be with her. I told her a story about a friend who worked as a trainee for Macy's last year and got to pull the Olive Oyl balloon. Every time they came to a windy cross street in Manhattan, Olive Oyl's enormous foot would be blown over the crowd, which would cower in terror. Gladys laughed and dropped off to sleep, woke up, was surprised to see me, and told me how thankful she was that I had come. And when was I shipping out again?

After working at our ministries (one novice worked in a homeless shelter, another in an AIDS hospice, another in the housing projects down the street, and another in a hospital), we returned home for a huge Thanksgiving meal prepared by Jerry and David, New England style—with oyster stuffing and brown bread. Before dinner we celebrated a Thanksgiving liturgy in the chapel, which in a few days we would decorate for Advent.

I fell head over heels in love with Advent—the liturgical season that precedes Christmas. Growing up, I had of course always enjoyed the Christmas season, but now the four weeks before December 25 were supplemented and nourished by the wonderful readings that we heard daily in Mass. The unexpected visit of the angel Gabriel and his sweet words of welcome to Mary. John the Baptist emerging from the wilderness to call Israel to repentance. Jeremiah telling of the good seed that would spring from the House of David. And, my favorite, the magnificent passages from Isaiah about the dry land becoming fertile, the valleys filled out, and the mountains being leveled:

> Then the eyes of the blind shall be opened,
> and the ears of the deaf unstopped;
> then the lame shall leap like a deer,
> and the tongue of the speechless sing for joy.

The beauty of these readings lent the many Christmas preparations in the novitiate—lighting the candles on the chapel's Advent wreath, buying gifts, and decorating the Christmas tree—more meaning, more heft, and infinitely more beauty.

In fact, I felt that way about the entire liturgical year, as we passed through Advent to Christmas to Lent to Easter to Pentecost to Ordinary Time, and returned again to Advent. The quiet progression of the liturgical year, which follows the life of Jesus, gave to my life a new meter, a new rhythm. During the year, our community encountered the great feasts and holy days of the Church, each of them with beautifully evocative readings at Mass. And after a few months in the novitiate, I began to look forward to the feast days of the saints, especially the Jesuits saints, when we would hear special prayers for them at Mass and, during the homilies, the stories of their lives.

On the third Sunday of Advent, the novices traveled to the province infirmary at Campion Center to sing carols for the older Jesuits. It was my first time in the infirmary and the first time back to Campion Center since my retreat in June. Though the Jesuits received excellent care, it was still hard to see so many elderly, sick men. "He was a wonderful teacher," said one of the nurses as she wheeled before me a priest crumpled by age and illness. It was sobering to think of the years of service that the Jesuits in the infirmary had given—and continued to give. I remembered the entry from the province catalog that listed their ministry as "Praying for the Society and the Church."

Indeed, the former general superior of the Jesuits, Pedro Arrupe, who had suffered a stroke, was at the time himself in a Jesuit infirmary in Rome awaiting death. "More than ever," he wrote shortly after his stroke:

> I find myself in the hands of God. This is what I have wanted all my life from my youth. But now there is a difference: now the initiative is entirely with God. It is indeed a profound spiritual experience to know and feel myself so totally in God's hands.

So it was with some emotion that we sang for these men. It was also clear that seeing novices gave many of them great pleasure. *Spes gregis,* one of the older Jesuits said when we entered his room: "The hope of the flock."

Some, though, were more difficult to please.

"Hello Fathah," said one of the nurses in her Boston accent. "The nawvices ah heah to sing carols for you!"

"Hello Father," we said.

"I'm the oldest Jesuit in the province!" said Father.

"That's nice," George said politely. George had worked for a few months in the infirmary as an orderly before he entered the novitiate. "Do you want to hear some carols, Father?"

"I'm the oldest Jesuit in the whole New England province. I'm ninety-four!"

"Uh-huh," said George. "Would you like to hear some Christmas carols?"

We waited.

"There used to be someone older than me." He paused. "But he's *dead!*"

He said this with such evident glee that we couldn't help laughing. This Jesuit was certainly not in need of carols. He had obviously derived enough Christmas cheer from his superannuated accomplishment.

A few days later, on a bitterly cold morning, the novices piled into a car and drove to a Trappist monastery in Spencer, a town about two hours west of Boston. I was excited about the trip, particularly after having read so much about the Trappists in Thomas Merton's books. Spencer, in fact, was founded as an offshoot of the Kentucky abbey to which Merton belonged. The novice director at Spencer had formerly been a Jesuit and, we learned, was also a convert from Judaism.

To support itself, St. Joseph's Abbey sold liturgical vestments as well as gourmet jams and jellies. The jams were sold in local supermarkets under the label "Trappist Preserves." I suggested we bring them a jar of peanut butter, and even made a little label saying "Jesuit Peanut Butter." This idea was nixed by the novice director. Instead, we brought them a small Christmas tree.

As it turned out, a tree was the last thing they needed. The stone monastery buildings stood on hundreds of acres of woodland which, in late December, were entirely blanketed with snow. Snow flurries blew about as we pulled up to the main entrance. It was a beautiful place, and I saw how conducive an environment like this could be to prayer.

We were given a tour of the monastery by one of the monks, clad in the distinctive black-and-white Trappist habit. I noticed he wasn't wearing socks on his sandaled feet. As we sat in the long stone chapter, or meeting, hall with him, he described the Trappist life of work and prayer: *Ora et labora.*

Afterwards, we joined the monks in the chapel for one of their daily prayers, chanted from the breviary. The combination of the cold weather, the peaceful stone buildings, the singing monks, and the beautiful prayer made me a little wistful that I hadn't joined the Trappists.

Christmas Eve and Christmas Day, spent at the novitiate, were much pleasanter than I had expected. Mass was celebrated on Christmas Eve after dinner. On Christmas Day we worked in our ministries and returned to a traditional Christmas dinner that Jerry and David had prepared for us. (I realized with some embarrassment that while I vigorously disapproved of *other*

Jesuit communities eating too well, I had no problem enjoying lavish feasts at the novitiate.) The next day I returned to Philadelphia for the first time since August. It was always good being home at Christmas, though my miniscule budget limited the amount of fabulous gifts I could give.

As soon as we returned after the New Year, the *secundi* began preparing for their "Long Experiment," which would take them to schools, parishes, and other full-time Jesuit works around the country for six months. Bill and I had learned that we would be going to work in Jamaica as our "Third World Experiment." The New England province had long sent both men and money to Jamaica. It was considered our "mission territory" and so, for the past few years, novices had traveled to the West Indies to work with the poor and experience life in a developing country. So the assignment was not a surprise.

The first-year class now included just Bill and me. In October, Emil, the Czech doctor, had announced that he would leave the novitiate to marry. Emil left to marry a woman with whom he had apparently never fallen out of love. None of us were surprised. Of all of the novices, Emil seemed the most secretive—quite an accomplishment in a community where you are required to share your faith life once a week. He announced his decision in conference one day and was gone within a few weeks.

January is also the month that most first-year Jesuit novices "make" the all-important "Long Retreat." Much of the first year builds up to the Spiritual Exercises. ("You'll understand this after the Long Retreat," was an almost daily refrain in conference.) But the novice director told me that, because I had had little experience in prayer before entering, I would make the retreat after returning from Jamaica. This meant another month of work in the hospital while Bill and the rest of the novices were away.

Jerry had made a very wise and careful decision, but I was still disappointed and feared that I might be failing as a novice. I dreaded telling people that I wasn't "ready" for the Long Retreat. What would they think? Though Jerry and David pointed out how self-defeating that kind of thinking was, I was still embarrassed.

So, after my *secundi* left for their Long Experiments and Bill left for the Long Retreat, I stayed behind to work at the hospital for a few more weeks. It was a different house, with the novices and the novitiate staff gone. I worked every day at Youville and came home for meals with the other Jesuits who remained in the community. Then, in late January, I made an eight-day retreat in Gloucester, to the same house where we had spent time during postulancy a few months earlier. The retreat was to prepare myself for the time in Jamaica.

That January, Gloucester presented a perfect New England winter scene. Snow, of course. And clear blue skies, frozen ponds, the cold Atlantic crashing against the rocks and, in town, weathered clapboard houses with fantastically long icicles hanging from the eaves. It was quite conducive to introspection.

It was also a good time for a retreat. Though I felt completely at home in the novitiate, there still were some things that troubled me. Heading off to live in Kingston, for one. During the past few months, I had heard enough horror stories from the *secundi* about the extreme poverty and the physical hardships in Kingston to grow increasingly fearful. I was especially concerned about the living conditions. Where would we live? In the slums? What was the food like? Were there doctors around if you fell ill? Was there malaria in Jamaica? Could you drink the water? I was especially worried that I would get sick on the Jamaican diet. What if there wasn't even any good food to eat? What if I would have to come home sick? That would be embarrassing, I thought dolefully.

On top of this, I was disappointed that things like this still bothered me. I was bothered that I was *bothered*. I expected that, after a few months as a novice, I would be more, well, detached, from things like this, and less fretful. (It was a good retreat, David told me afterwards, but I was still the same person!)

The way I saw it, I always reacted to difficult situations in a purely human way—with fear and anxiety. Only much later, after some prayer and direction, would I gradually see where God was in my feelings and desires and worries. But why couldn't I see that immediately and skip all the worrying? Why couldn't I see God in situations immediately? I wanted, I guess, to become more aware of God as things occurred. I wanted a living experience of God's presence. I remember thinking that this must be how saints experience God—*as* they lived life, not just in retrospect.

An older Jesuit named Joe lived with us at the novitiate. I thought him holy in this very way, in his ability to find God in the present. Joe always seemed so free: very balanced and "detached"—in a good way—from all the unimportant things in life. And he had a great sense of humor when it came to life's little problems. One day he described sitting on an airport tarmac in Boston for five hours, stuck in a plane without air-conditioning. The plane took off twice, circled, and landed back in the airport. Now, had that been *me*, I would have been boiling over with frustration, wondering when we would leave or what was wrong. Joe, on the other hand, laughed as he related his saga and remarked how funny it was to him as it was happening. For Joe, life, even when difficult, seemed full of funny things like that. God always seemed very present to him.

The week after my retreat, I was sitting in the living room reading the newspaper. Joe came in and asked me if I was looking forward to my time in Jamaica.

"Not really," I admitted sheepishly. I decided to be honest. "I'm pretty nervous." And I explained to him my embarrassing fear of getting sick in Jamaica. "I'm afraid I won't be able to make it. I mean, what if I have to come home? I would be so embarrassed . . . "

He listened intently and said, "Well, why not just allow yourself to get sick?"

His insight was so liberating; it was just what I needed to hear. He meant, of course, that I was trying too hard to be perfect. So *what* if I got sick and wasn't the "perfect" Jesuit? It would be part of the experience, he said. Joe's insight helped me feel a little more relaxed about the next few months.

On February 15, Bill and I left for Jamaica. It was my first time in the Caribbean, and I enjoyed the airplane trip that took us first over Cuba and then the aquamarine waters surrounding Jamaica. Bill and I sang Beach Boys songs as we prepared for our four-month stay.

8.
Simple Tasks

*My task was simplified as soon as I realized
that I could do nothing by myself.*

St. Thérèse of Lisieux, *Story of a Soul.*

When we landed at the Kingston airport late on a sunny afternoon, we were met by two young Jesuits. Norman Manley Airport is a distinctly tropical place, with magenta and orange bougainvillaea plants spilling over the white stucco walls, and tall palm trees alive with brightly colored chattering birds. Once we left the airport and turned onto the main road, however, it was a different story—and a shock: my first sight of a city gripped by poverty. Trash, mangy goats, huge pigs, rotting garbage, busy vendors, burned-out cars, traffic. And the smells: burning garbage, factory smoke, body odor, and kerosene. The smells of the developing world.

We were driven to the Jesuit high school, called St. George's College. It is a compound set squarely in the middle of a sprawling Kingston ghetto, surrounded with nine-foot stone walls topped with razor wire. The walls encompassed playing fields, stucco classroom buildings capped with terra cotta roofs, enormous palm trees and, in the middle of it all, the Jesuit residence—a dozen or so rooms built around a gracious atrium boasting hibiscus bushes, day lilies, and four towering palm trees, whose broad leaves extended over the roof. In the center of the courtyard stood a stone statue of Jesus pointing to his heart. During the day, the sun shone into the atrium and gave the place a bright, clean, airy feel. And when it rained the drops hit the clay tile roof with a sharp staccato sound not unlike gunfire.

But this was not where I was to live. Instead, Bill and I were assigned to a concrete annex built in the 1960s. Despite the often stunning natural beauty around us—palm trees, etc.— I found the living situation pretty grim. The annex hadn't been used as a residence for a few years and was now used primarily for classroom space, except for our floor, which was reserved for guests. In the open hallways were piles of moldy books and rusted desk chairs. The floor of the common bathroom was covered with the dry leaves and dead insects that had lately blown in through the broken windows. My own room featured an astonishing array of wildlife: mosquitoes, lizards, moths, and a bees' nest located neatly under the top sill of my window.

I asked the superior of the community about this, a friendly but bluff Jesuit.

"Uh, there's a bees' nest in my room."

"And?" he said.

And? I thought it was pretty obvious.

"And I want to get rid of it."

"How big is it?"

"It's small I guess . . . but well . . . I don't much like having bees flying around in my room." I was growing frustrated. "Can I have some bug spray? Do you have Raid here?"

He considered this for a moment. "I tell you what. Why don't you wait until it gets bigger so we can knock it down more easily?"

Was I, I wondered, being too American or was trying to share my room with bees ridiculous? Maybe I wasn't being accepting enough. I thought about it for a few seconds and decided: I want an insect-free room. After searching the house unsuccessfully for bug spray, I ended up standing on a chair and spraying some shaving cream on the offending nest which, though not deadly, covered the bees with a sufficient quantity of lather to cause them to fall to the ground, where I scooped them up and tossed them out the window. So much for inculturation.

The first night, I lay on top of the ancient metal bed and listened to the sounds of raucous reggae music blaring from the local bars, barking dogs, gunshots, screeching lizards, and the hum of innumerable mosquitoes. God. What was I *doing* here? I thought about my nice, air-conditioned office at GE.

The next morning I awoke feeling not at all refreshed but at least grateful that I had lasted a night.

Fortunately, there was a group of about a dozen young Jesuits—both Americans and Jamaicans—in communities throughout Kingston with whom Bill and I became great friends. Every month we would meet for faith sharing and a meal. The Jamaican Jesuits had seen their share of timid, skittish American novices, and deftly shepherded us through our first homesick weeks—squiring Bill and me around Kingston and the rest of the island. And since the American Jesuits had faced similar experiences, they assured me that it was quite natural to miss the worldly, creature comforts of the States.

There was also a group of energetic young lay volunteers living in Kingston who were friends of the young S.J.s. The Jesuit International Volunteers, all recent college graduates, spent a few years in Kingston working in schools and social agencies. Though they were years younger than I, they already had a year in Jamaica under their belts, and they tooled around Kingston like natives. "I really admire what you're doing," one of them said to me on the porch at St. George's early in my stay. It was all I could do to keep from laughing. In my mind, it was they—living on their own and fending for themselves without the support of a religious community—who were the adventurous ones.

Bill and I spent a few days casting about for work. The first place we visited was an orphanage a stone's throw away from St. George's, run by the Sisters of Mercy. The Alpha Boys' School is a home for those known in Jamaica as "bad boys," that is, problem children.

When we walked into the large compound, we encountered hundreds of barefoot boys running around a dirt playing field, wearing identical blue shirts and dirty, ripped shorts. Sister Regine, the effervescent principal of the school, said that she would love to have us work as "recreation sponsors" which, as far as I could tell, meant that we would be responsible for seeing that the boys didn't hurt one other during soccer games. Just last week, she remarked, one of the boys had put someone's eye out with a sharp stick. Or, she said, we could help out by tutoring. Perhaps inordinately attached to my own eyesight, I volunteered to help out as a tutor.

The one venue the novice director had asked us to "strongly consider" for our work was a hospice for the sick and dying run by the Missionaries of Charity. The hospice was founded to care for the people who would otherwise die on the streets of Kingston. The sisters were very welcoming and said that they would need us to bathe the old men. They themselves were happy to bathe the women but balked at bathing men, and the one Jamaican man the sisters employed was terribly overworked. I decided that if I had to work at Mother Teresa's hospice around so much death, I would also work at the orphanage, where it seemed like there was a lot of life.

Part of our first week also included a sort of official orientation with other new religious, priests, and lay volunteers, arranged by the Catholic Archdiocese of Kingston. We were treated to some exceedingly dull lectures about the country's political situation, the economic hardships of the Jamaicans and, finally, a more personal overview of the history of the Church in Jamaica, compliments of the archbishop of Kingston.

I had already heard about this archbishop, who was also a New England Jesuit. New England had, in the past few decades, sent dozens of missionaries to Jamaica and had, in return, received some Jamaican vocations. One of these men eventually became the archbishop. Samuel Emanuel Carter strode into the room in his white cassock with red piping, which looked striking against his dark skin. Though he spoke energetically for two hours, I dozed off in the warm room.

Finally, he concluded his talk and announced, "Now we will all pray the *Memorare*."

The what?

Everyone stood. The sound of chairs scraping against the concrete floor woke me. I leapt to my feet.

Of course, I had no idea what the *Memorare* was, and was mortified when everyone shouted out the beginning of the prayer: "Remember, O Most Gracious Virgin Mary . . . " The archbishop looked at me pointedly as I stood dumbly through the rest of the prayer. Unfortunately, it's a long prayer (and one that's hard to fake), so His Grace had ample time to consider the sorry state of contemporary Jesuit formation.

After a week or so, I settled down to something of a routine. At night I lit a small green mosquito coil that quickly filled my room with an acrid smoke that kept away the many mosquitoes. (There were, of course, no screens.) When the coil gave out after six hours, the mosquitoes began biting, and I knew it was morning. This proved far more effective than any alarm clock. But even if I slept through the mosquito alarm, the sun, which shot up high in the sky at 6:00, would wake me. There was hardly any dawn or dusk in Jamaica. When the sun rose, it was instantly day; when the sun fell, the island was plunged into darkness.

If I felt adventurous in the morning, I would take a cold shower in the hall bathroom. The shower head had fallen off, so I positioned myself under a stream of cold water that ran out in a desultory manner from a steel pipe sticking out of the tiled wall. Usually, though, I wandered over to the main Jesuit residence where they (usually) had hot water. This meant walking through the school compound, a towel and shampoo in hand, under the watchful eyes of the students. There were a number of lizards who resided in the bathrooms in the main building, so often I showered with a baleful eye fixed on a lizard slowly crawling across the ceiling, hoping that he wouldn't decide to jump down and join me for morning ablutions. Breakfast was tea, an orange, and toast with guava jelly.

In the afternoons I walked the few blocks to the Alpha Boys' School and wandered into the classrooms. The teacher would select one of the students, and I would spend an hour with him, helping him with his lessons. Together we'd sit on a wooden bench in the Jamaican sun and struggle through reading or "maths." Typically the teachers would assign me six or seven students each afternoon. We wrote on the used scraps of paper that blew around the yard and, later, a small chalkboard. Because most of the boys had severe learning problems—some of them were mentally handicapped—I often grew sad in the face of their struggles. Many did not know the alphabet, a few couldn't spell their own name, the majority were unable to do basic arithmetic.

But I was happy to be around so many young people who laughed a lot and clearly enjoyed being pulled out of class. My two favorites were Duane and Ricaldo. Duane was a tiny six-year-old boy. We spent most of our time working on his maths. Whenever he was selected for tutoring, he jumped out of his seat and ran over to me, grinning, and put his hand in mine. One day, helping him with his sums, I noticed that his tiny bitten-down fingernails were a bright red. "What did you do to your fingernails, Duane?" I asked.

"I painted me fingers red, Brother!"

"How come?"

He held out both hands and screwed up his face.

"Because it's *pretty!*"

Ricaldo, eighteen years old and nearly illiterate, could be enticed to read if the story was particularly violent. Of course, I felt sheepish about offering him stories of murder and mayhem (he liked almost anything to do with pirates) but decided it was worth it to get him to read. One story included a blood-thirsty pirate who had killed someone by "thrusting his sword into his enemy up to the hilt." We looked up "hilt" in the dictionary together; Ricaldo's eyes widened when he realized the spectacular dimensions of the pirate's accomplishment.

Ricaldo's reading progressed rapidly and his face lit up in a smile when anyone complimented him on his reading skills.

Eventually, I saved up enough money to buy him an entire book of pirate stories entitled *Henry Morgan, the Buccaneer,* which he kept in a small cardboard box under his bed to read at night.

It was sobering to realize that some of the Alpha boys would probably be worse off after they "graduated" from the school. The sisters did a superb job of educating the kids, but after the age of eighteen, the boys left the school to try to make a life on their own. But in Kingston, where poverty and unemployment ruled, it would be almost impossible to earn a living.

During the mornings, I walked from the Jesuit residence through one of the slums on my way to Mother Teresa's hospice. On the way through the steamy streets, I would pass the hundreds of Jamaican children on their way to school—boys in khaki pants and white shirts, girls in white shirts and brightly colored jumpers. And by the side of the roads, all sorts of activity: people bathing, brushing their teeth, and laundering clothes in the open air. Young men leaned aimlessly against corrugated metal shacks where stout Jamaican women sold fruits, fish, sodas, and cheap candy. There was garbage everywhere. Since I was conspicuous as the only white man around, I was greeted by almost everyone. "Good morning, Father!"

When I arrived for my first day of work at Our Lady Queen of Peace, I was quite bowled over by the smell. Excrement, disinfectant, garbage, bleach, tea, urine, and cooking all mixed into one overpowering, almost tangible scent. The sisters kept the place immaculate, but it smelled foul nonetheless.

It was something of a thrill to work with the Missionaries of Charity, whose striped white-and-blue saris, made famous by Mother Teresa of Calcutta, were familiar even to me. They were joyful and obviously loved their work. They laughed constantly. And this was no mean feat: by the time I arrived at 9:00 in the morning, the sisters had been up for hours, having worked all morning bathing the women and preparing breakfast for the residents. In the afternoon, the sisters set out to clean the houses of people too weak or sick to do so themselves. In the midst of this, they found time for an hour of prayer and Mass. And when a priest came to celebrate Mass, the sisters fixed him an elaborate meal, in stark contrast to the simple fare they ate—the leftovers from the patients' food.

Initially, I was skeptical of their almost preternatural cheerfulness, which I suspected to be some sort of denial of the death and suffering around them. I was certain that anyone who was this sunny in such a milieu must be faking it. But like their foundress, Mother Teresa, they really *did* seem to find joy in their work and in their ability to help people face death peacefully. At least in this particular community, the happiness was genuine.

But for me, it was almost unbearable. The work at Youville Hospital looked easy in comparison. My "job description" at the hospice was pretty simple: clean and bathe old men. I would usually help a man into the large bathroom, struggle to pull off his dirty or excrement-filled pants, strip off his smelly shirt, and help him into the shower, where I would wash him. Or I would wash the men on a rickety metal chair with a toilet seat fastened to its top; this way the dirty water could run into the rusted drain at the center of the painted concrete floor.

One old man, named Ezekiel, was blind. It took some doing to help him from his seat, steer him to the bathroom, sit him on the metal chair, remove his clothes, guide him into the shower, reach around him and turn on the water without knocking him over, wash him, dry him in the shower without getting myself soaked and, finally, get him back into his clothes, which I had to be careful not to get wet during his shower. Often, in the middle of these maneuvers, he would blow his nose using his index finger. Quick reflexes were required to stay out of his firing range.

I dreaded going to work. The length of my morning walks to the hospice were proportionate to how much I wanted to avoid working that day. One day I was told by the sisters to clip the men's toenails, which had grown so long and hard that they said no one but me could clip them. (It was all I could do to keep from saying, "Oh *thanks!*") Of course, the toenails were part of their smelly toes which, in turn, were part of their spectacularly smelly feet. I had to wash their feet first before I could bring myself to clip their toenails.

Clipping fingernails was only slightly less repulsive. But at least I was doing something useful. Sometimes, after I had washed everyone, I felt somewhat useless—as I did at Youville—so I chatted with the men. One guy called over and asked me to clip his nails. They looked as if they hadn't been clipped for a few months. After I finished, he rubbed his fingers together and said, "But Brother, you need to do me nails again. They are too *scratchy!*"

I returned to my charge, clipped his nails even shorter, and moved on to someone else who had called out from across the room, "Clip me nails, Brother! Clip me nails!"

From across the room, the first man shouted once again: "Brother, they are still too *scratchy.* You need to file them!"

This was a bit much. "I don't even file my *own* nails!" I said. All the men laughed.

So why didn't all of this feel more, well . . . spiritual? The Missionaries of Charity didn't seem to mind when someone vomited on them or soiled their pants. Or if they minded, they didn't complain about it. One morning the superior pulled me aside. "Brother Jim, I want to show you something." She led me into a small room where a man sat with his throat wrapped in a bloodstained bandage. She slowly unwound the bandage. "This man has throat cancer. We should pray for him." I couldn't bear to look, but I could smell his disease, the smell of death. And I felt sad and guilty that he repulsed me.

I realized that if I saw this same scene as part of, say, a movie, I would probably find it terribly moving. I would sit in the movie theater thinking, "Wow, I should be doing that." So now that I *was* doing it, why didn't I feel moved? One morning, while washing one of the men, I thought that if this were in fact a movie, there would doubtless be some stirring background music. Maybe that's what was missing. So I started singing to myself when I worked. Mostly religious songs to get me in the mood and take my mind off of people blowing snot all over me. Eventually, the patients hummed along with me.

One day a sister told me that one of the men was about to die and needed to be baptized. He was one of the men that I used to like working with. I didn't even mind bathing him—he was so friendly and talkative. The sisters wanted me to baptize him.

I protested. I was not a priest and the sisters were more qualified than I was. (And I suspected they turned to me because I was a man.) They were certainly holier than I was.

"Oh, but Brother," they said, "you have been working with him. He knows *you*. You must do it."

The sisters led me to the room where he lay in bed wheezing, all skin and bones. Food was encrusted around his mouth, he had obviously just soiled himself; there was a strong stench. Though normally he could move around fairly well, today he was almost completely immobile. A wave of pity swept over me. One of the sisters and I sat him up and propped him up in our arms. I could feel the fragile bones moving under his dry skin; it was like holding a baby bird. A few sisters gathered around, and one handed me a plastic cup of water and a bent spoon.

"What do you want to call him, Brother?" Still at a loss I hesitated, but finally said that I thought we might baptize him Joseph. I poured the water over his head with the crumpled spoon and it trickled down, wetting his thin pajamas. It was an immensely sad moment but one that seemed to fill everyone in the room—especially Joseph—with great peace. Afterwards, the sisters and I went back to our tasks. Joseph died a few days later.

I never got over the physical repulsion of working at Mother Teresa's hospice. But gradually I was able to bear the work by discovering compassion for the people living there. It used to help to think of Jesus suffering. It certainly didn't make the work any more pleasant, and I questioned the wisdom of pretending I was helping Jesus rather than the people before me, but at least it was helping me do what I had been missioned to do (along with the humming).

One morning, while I was walking back from the hospice, a woman called to me from her small house and asked if I could come into her house to "pray." She was around thirty-five, obese, and looked as if she hadn't been outside for some time. Her red eyes signaled many sleepless nights.

As soon as I entered her house, she began weeping. She had no job, no money, and no food, she said. And she was having terrible nightmares. I started crying, too, so sad was her situation. I took her hand and prayed with her and told her—what else could I say?—that it was okay to feel afraid. We prayed that God might help her with her problems, and I told her to look out for me in the mornings. From then on, I used to stop into her house to check up on her and chat. Unexpected moments and meetings like this helped to put my own minor struggles in Jamaica in perspective.

And just when it seemed like I had had it with clipping toenails at Mother Teresa's, there was usually a well-timed break. The presence of so many younger Jesuits and young volunteers insured that there were plenty of opportunities to get away on the weekends. We were, after all, in Jamaica. One day we took a ride up into the cool Blue Mountains and passed a car, full of waving passengers. It was the Missionaries of Charity off on a picnic! I teased them mercilessly the next day for slacking off. "We worked twice as hard the day before to get ready, Brother," they said. And I had no doubt that they had.

There was also a fine movie theater in Kingston, an immense palace called the Carib. The show invariably began with coming attractions for Ninja movies and Indian films. These were followed by advertisements for exterminating companies in Kingston. "Do you have *these?*" said the announcer as a nine-foot roach filled the screen. (Yes I do, actually.) One night, a few of us went to see *The Mighty Quinn*, with Denzel Washington as a Jamaican police officer. The crowd howled at Hollywood's version of Jamaica and at Denzel's Caribbean accent.

And though we were far from the more exotic resorts in northern Jamaica, there were plenty of secluded beaches an hour or so away. My very favorite spot was a tiny island called Lime Cay. To get there, you first hopped a ferry to Port Royal, a former hangout for pirates, south of the city. Once in Port Royal, you had to hunt down a local fisherman willing to take you in his battered boat to Lime Cay. You climbed into the small boat (which seated only three or four people), on went the outboard motor, and off you went skipping over the perfect blue water towards what seemed like the open Caribbean. In a few minutes, you would spy slender palm trees and, soon, a small white island.

The island itself was no bigger than a city block, and nothing more than white sand, brush, and palm trees. The fisherman would leave with promises to return when the sun set. And you could be certain that he would indeed return: he wasn't paid until he did. Still, it seemed quite adventurous to be on a deserted island with no way of returning home.

We spent the afternoons lunching and snorkeling and swimming in the warm waters. It was perfectly relaxing. At one point, lying on the warm sand looking into the clear blue vault, I wondered if I would ever feel this relaxed again, and what I might have been doing at GE had I stayed. And I suddenly remembered the relaxation exercises with the biofeedback doctor in Stamford. I was finally here, on the desert island that I could never imagine!

Along with the younger Jesuits, there were a few older, more colorful ones in the St. George's community who had lived and worked in Kingston for years. One father, for example, rather than washing his underwear, used to air it out on a line outside of his room. He also used to clean his ears with his napkin during meals. I tried politely to avoid sitting with him at dinner.

Another father's chief joy in life seemed to be his cat, Samantha. Whenever she would get lost, he would stand at the door of the Jesuit residence and yell, "Samaaaantha!" to the great amusement of the Jamaican students.

I got along swimmingly with Gerry, an old missionary who shared my love of movies. A few blocks away, in the middle of one of Kingston's slums was an unlikely video rental store located in the owner's living room. You climbed up the stairs of his house, passed through his kitchen—where his mother was usually busy cooking—and finally entered the living room, where thousands of video cassettes were laid out on sofas, chairs, tables, any available space. Every single one was a pirated video that had somehow found its way to his living room. Some had warnings that would appear as you screened the movie: "If you are watching this tape, it is an illegal copy. Call this number . . . " Others had apparently been filmed in theaters while the movies were shown; you could see people getting up and down, occasionally you would hear laughter or applause. The scholastics at St. George's might rent one or two for a weekend, and Gerry was always the first in the TV room.

Early in my stay, I noticed Gerry reading the published letters of Evelyn Waugh. I told him how much I enjoyed *Brideshead Revisited,* and he offered me his book after he had finished. Years ago, Gerry said, the archbishop of Jamaica asked him to escort Evelyn Waugh around the island. The author had come to see his friend, Nöel Coward, who lived in a house called "Firefly," in Port Antonio. Gerry squired him around for a few weeks.

What was Waugh like? I asked. "He was a real pill," he said. And then he whispered conspiratorially, "I think he was a *homo*, too."

One morning around Eastertime, I sat in a rocking chair on the wide porch of the Jesuit residence reading one of Gerry's Evelyn Waugh books, as the parakeets chattered from their perches in one of the tall pine trees that shaded the house. I heard from the cathedral, which stood but a few paces from the school, Easter songs drifting about in the warm Jamaican air, and I thought quite suddenly—Hey, I'm happy! It was something of a surprise, after the weeks of struggling, and an entirely pleasant one at that.

Later that month, I sat on the porch reading an old *Time* magazine. In it was an article on time. Americans have less and less free time, it said, and fewer opportunities to reflect on their hectic lives. It was difficult not to think, sitting on the porch at St. George's, how lucky I was to be doing the kind of work I was doing and have the time to appreciate it. Toenails and all.

I never stopped worrying about getting sick, though there were only a few times when I actually did get sick. And I began to realize the futility of worrying about the "what ifs" in life. My spiritual director in Jamaica suggested I should pay more attention to the present than to the future. Being more attentive to the present meant that I could better see and appreciate all that God was giving me *now*—like Lime Cay, the Alpha boys, the Missionaries of Charity, and my friends in Kingston—rather than worrying about what *might* go wrong in the future. The good times really did seem to outnumber the bad in Jamaica and towards the end, I realized I'd miss the place. That seemed to be the lesson to take away from Jamaica. Tomorrow, as Jesus said, has enough problems of its own.

Towards the end of my stay, as I was riding with one of the scholastics in a mini-bus up to his community in another part of Kingston, he told me a story of a New England novice from a few years back. Apparently, said novice was so distraught with the living conditions at St. George's—the bugs, the noise, and all that—that after one night in the Jesuit community, he marched into the superior's office and announced that he was leaving: leaving the community, leaving Jamaica, and leaving the Jesuits. He was gone in a few days. So I guessed that I hadn't done so badly after all.

At the close of our time there—around the end of May—the Jesuits and the volunteers threw a party for Bill and me on the roof of the Jesuit residence. The party, which lasted into the wee hours, also provided me with an unexpected going-away gift.

In college I was a pot smoker of the recreational, weekend kind. And Jamaican pot was always reputed to be the best. So, before I left Boston, I asked the novice director if one could smoke pot in Jamaica. I had meant was it *legal*, not would he give me permission. Either way, the answer was a firm no. One of the scholastics shook his head dolefully when I related my story, and gave me some advice. "When it comes to stuff like that in religious life," he said, "always remember that it's easier to ask for forgiveness than for permission."

So there I was in Jamaica—Land of Ganja—unable to smoke. I mentioned this to one of the volunteers a few weeks before leaving. What a waste! he said. That night on the roof he smiled slyly and whispered, "I have a present for you." He reached into his pocket and carefully pulled out a joint. "I know you're not supposed to, but it wouldn't it be a waste not to use it?" I didn't need much convincing.

Earlier in the day, I stopped by Mother Teresa's to say goodbye to the sisters and the patients and to take some photos. "Come back, Brother! Come back to work with us again!" I would miss the sisters and the people at the hospice. The work itself, though, I was happy to have completed.

It was even harder saying goodbye to the Alpha boys, as I knew that I would probably never see them again. Even if I returned to Jamaica at some point in the future, their lives would probably have led them to the streets of Kingston. I brought a camera to take pictures of the boys I had spent time with. They came spilling out of the classrooms, mugging outrageously. "Take me picture, Brother!" "When are you coming back, Brother?" Ricaldo covered his face in embarrassment when I took a photo, but made me promise to send him a copy.

On May 31, Bill and I flew back to Boston. It was good to be back in the States, land of unlimited hot showers, plentiful window screens, and good food. I noticed that there were certainly a lot of white people around, too. (And everyone seemed so well dressed.) Yet, surprisingly, I realized that, even with all the frustrations I encountered there, I'd actually *like* to return to Jamaica at some point. And I also hoped that I wouldn't forget what I had learned there.

But there wasn't much danger of forgetting anything, because I plunged almost immediately into the Long Retreat, an experience that draws heavily on both imagination and memory. On June 30, I returned again to Gloucester which, after postulancy and retreat days, was for me a place that seemed suffused with the presence of God.

EVERY JESUIT makes a Long Retreat twice in his life, during novitiate and at the very end of his formation. The Long Retreat, or Thirty-Day Retreat, follows St. Ignatius Loyola's *Spiritual Exercises*, which is essentially a retreat director's handbook. Ignatius wrote the *Exercises*, the result of his own experiences in prayer, as a series of meditations—exercises—to enable people to follow God more closely.

The retreat house at Gloucester was booked solid with people making the Long Retreat. Plenty of sisters, a few priests and deacons, and many lay people. I was the only Jesuit novice. Most of the lay people were, not surprisingly, active in their local parishes and had been praying and making retreats for years. For many, making the Long Retreat at Gloucester was the fulfillment of a longtime dream.

The retreat staff hosted a welcoming dinner for the retreatants in the dining room on the night we arrived. Since people are invariably friendly on retreats, everyone quickly got acquainted. I wondered, though, what the point was, since the next day we were going to be silent. But no matter. "I'll pray for you!" everyone said.

David, the assistant novice director, came to Gloucester to direct me, while the rest of the novices remained at Arrupe House on the summer *ordo*, which included some apostolic work as well as studying Spanish. David also had a number of other "directees," or retreatants, who met with him during the retreat. He would stay in the Jesuit community attached to the retreat house. My own room was in the two-story dormitory extension to the main house, in a long, green-tiled corridor of about twenty rooms. Each room had a large picture window that afforded a view of the ocean, a single bed, and a narrow Formica countertop running along the length of the window that served as a desk. Mass was celebrated every afternoon at 5:00. The remainder of the day was spent in silence.

The first week began with two meditations: first on God's love and second on our limitations and tendency toward sin. On the first day of the retreat, David asked me just to relax and enjoy the beauty of creation.

This was awfully easy to do during a summer in Gloucester. The waves crashed on the rocks a few hundred yards away from the house. Lobster boats ventured forth every morning as seagulls and black cormorants swarmed about them. Around the large fresh-water pond a few feet from the house, red-winged blackbirds sang, a new brood of ducklings paddled around with their parents and turtles sunned themselves lazily on the dark, mossy rocks. By the docks in town, the Gloucester fishermen sat in their wooden boats and patiently mended nets. And at night, over the rocks, the moon set, a vivid orange. It wasn't difficult to see the goodness of God surrounding us. Neither was it difficult to see where he had been good to me in my life. I thanked God for the blessings he had given me over the years: my family, my friends, and now my Jesuit vocation.

Nor was it difficult to see my sinfulness. David asked me to read Psalm 51, which placed my sinfulness squarely before me:

> Have mercy on me, O God,
> according to your steadfast love;
> according to your abundant mercy
> blot out my transgressions.
> Wash me thoroughly from my iniquity,
> and cleanse me from my sin.
>
> For I know my transgressions,
> and my sin is ever before me.

I spent almost a whole week in prayer confronting my own demons, and my imperfect human nature: my desire to have everyone think highly of me; my tendency to judge and to gossip; my need to do everything for praise. After having spent so much time being introspective in the novitiate, it was easy to recognize my shortcomings, which I began to bitterly regret. And I resented not having been able to overcome them more easily. By the end of the week, I felt a total shit, and so it was easy to pray, when David asked me to, on the passage of the woman caught in adultery, from the Gospel of John. But while I felt my own sinfulness intensely, I could also, by imagining myself as the woman in the story, feel Jesus' surprising and powerful forgiveness.

Despite the *sturm und drang* of prayer, life at Gloucester was almost sinfully relaxing and, after a few days, I happily settled into the rhythm of the retreat. Breakfast first, then prayer.

David had asked me to pray three or four times a day, for an hour at a time. At first, I wondered if I could do this for thirty straight days. And at times, particularly when my prayer was dry, I found it hard to continue and kept checking my watch as I shifted around anxiously on the prayer pillows in the chapel. Fifteen minutes to go. Ten minutes to go. My butt started to hurt from sitting for so many hours a day. Gradually, however, my butt (and the rest of me) grew accustomed to it. God, I discovered, gives people the patience and graces they need on a retreat.

After morning prayer came a long walk into Gloucester, first past the pond, where I checked out whatever was swimming or crawling or flying around. Then past the tonier houses of Gloucester, past the marina, where the fishing boats sat waiting to be repaired, past the inner harbor and, finally, to my usual destination: the enormous bronze statue of the Gloucester Fisherman, a monument to the men who died plying their trade. He stands with his hand firmly on the wheel, clad in a slicker, looking resolutely out to sea. On the stone pedestal, a haunting legend—*They that go down to the sea in ships*—from Psalm 107:

> They that go down to the sea in ships,
> that do business in great waters;
> these see the works of the Lord,
> and his wonders in the deep.

I returned before lunch, where I could sit by the Atlantic and write and draw in a little leather notebook my sister had given me. Meals were taken in silence but, because you couldn't have fifty people chomping on food and clanking silverware, soft music was played over the loudspeakers in the dining room. Everyone sat on the same side of the tables, the better to look out of the big picture windows at the ocean.

After lunch came another hour of prayer in the chapel (along with a dozen or so other people) or in a small and sunny room they called the "Mary Chapel," which had served as the solarium in the old house. It was a small room with a cool, terra cotta floor and pink and rose cushions pushed against the walls. In the corner, a polychrome statue of Mary stood atop a wrought-iron flowerpot stand that held pots of flourishing African violets. There was plenty of light for them, since the Mary Chapel occupied a corner of the house whose two walls were entirely taken up by tall windows that faced the ocean. It was the ideal spot for prayer.

After that, a very long walk or a bike ride. There were all sorts of interesting paths near the retreat house. You could scramble over the huge granite rocks in front of the house and sit by the ocean, walk around the pond, or amble along the beach. My favorite walk was to the lighthouse about a mile away. A stone jetty jutted from a red-and-white striped lighthouse into the ocean, and you could sit and watch fishermen casting their lines and reeling in their catch. I spent one afternoon there meditating on Jesus' exhortation to the apostles by the Sea of Galilee: "Come and I will make you fishers of people."

Stray dogs usually patrolled the path to the lighthouse so, just in case, I started carrying a big stick that I had found in the fields surrounding the retreat house. A Franciscan sister who was seeing David for direction told him that I reminded her of John the Baptist as I wandered around with my staff. (This, apparently, was the passage in the Gospel she was praying about that morning.) Since the Franciscans are big on animals, David didn't have the heart to tell her that I was carrying the stick as a weapon to use against any unruly dogs.

Mail was a big deal. The directors left any letters or cards for the retreatants on a large marble table that stood in the main hall. I checked it about fifteen times a day. I knew I would occasionally be bored, so I had asked my friends to write. I told Rob about the retreat and that I would certainly need some letters, given that I wouldn't be able to talk for thirty days.

"Like the Odd Couple," he exclaimed when I told him.
Excuse me?

"The Odd Couple!" he said. "When they went to that monastery."

Rob reminded me that on a particular episode of the television show *The Odd Couple*, Felix and Oscar visit a monastery where dozens of taciturn monks wander around in brown robes and sandals. Silence is enforced so strictly that even visitors—like Felix and Oscar—are punished severely for talking. In order to prevent the pair from talking, both receive a little blackboard. When Oscar breaks the silence by calling his bookie, Felix, of course, feels obliged to report him to the abbot. Oscar gets in trouble and writes a message to Felix on his little blackboard: "Thou shalt not fink!" So, during the second week of retreat, I found a heavy envelope sitting on the mail table bearing Rob's return address. Inside was a tiny blackboard, and written in chalk, "Thou shalt not fink!"

The second and third weeks of the retreat focused on the life of Christ. Throughout the *Spiritual Exercises*, Ignatius encourages an active use of the imagination, to picture oneself in various scenes from Scripture, which he calls "composition of place." In the meditation on the Nativity, for example, you ask God to help you imagine yourself in the stable during the Nativity, with Mary and Joseph—seeing what they see, smelling what they smell, and hearing what they hear. I took to this method of prayer readily and found it extremely fruitful. In the midst of this contemplation, you naturally and spontaneously experience all kinds of surprising emotions and insights which, in turn, can help you draw closer to God.

I enjoyed imagining the different episodes centering on Christ's life, beginning with the Annunciation in the Gospel of Luke, one of my favorite passages in Scripture. Thinking about Mary's ability to say "yes" to God brought forth all sorts of images and questions and ideas. Where did Mary's great faith come from? Why was it that God chose such a humble person? What gave her the courage to say "yes" to such an awesome responsibility? What was the meaning of Mary's virginity? Just that one meditation kept me busy for a few days, continually yielding new insights about how God was at work in Mary's life, and in mine.

With most of the meditations, whether it was Jesus' parables, his miracles, his time with his disciples, or his crucifixion, the same things kept coming up in prayer: my pride, my impatience, my sinfulness, and how they kept me from drawing closer to God. But at the same time, I realized how God had stuck by me all along, despite my shortcomings. I thought about how I always worried, worried, worried . . . about getting sick in Jamaica, winning the respect of people, not being able to "do" things in the hospital, about everything. But no matter how worried I was about a situation, God was always there, beside me . . . waiting for me.

We had two "break" days, when the retreatants were able to talk with one another and be a little active in the midst of all the contemplation: we could go to the beach, go into Gloucester, or visit nearby Rockport, a former fishing village now packed with shops, restaurants, and tourists. A group of us went out to dinner on one break day to a local seafood restaurant and were nearly kicked out, we were so loud. Two weeks of bottled-up conversation. Strangely, I felt as if I knew everyone. Praying together, even in silence, had made us into a community of sorts.

Sometimes the days dragged, and I felt surprisingly tired from so much prayer. Contemplation, it turned out, was hard work, requiring a great deal of concentration. But most of the time, feeling so near to God, I was conscious of how lucky I was to have this opportunity. After all, how many people get a whole month off to pray? I never had so much time to think and reflect on my own. By the end of the retreat, I felt closer to God than ever and more certain that it was as a Jesuit that I could best serve God and find peace.

On the final day of retreat, I packed up my few things and said my goodbyes to the retreatants, surprised at how close I felt to all of them. I really *had* felt them praying for me through the retreat. It was the last day of July, the first day for the novices' vacation time, or "villa." I would spend a week at my parents' house and a week with the other novices at a rented house on Cape Cod.

David drove me to South Station in Boston, and I boarded a crowded, noisy Amtrak train bound for New York, where I would spend a night on a pull-out bed in Rob's apartment. I fell asleep almost immediately in my seat and woke up just a few minutes before the train pulled into New York. And after thirty days of meditations on the life of Christ, composition of place, prayer, and silence by the sea, I stepped off the train and was swallowed up by the jostling, noisy crowds that swirled and eddied about Penn Station.

9.

Seeing Life Whole

*Conversion is not a giving away of something that we can
well afford to lose. It goes much deeper than that. It is a
putting away of something that we are: our old self with its
all-too-human, all-too-worldly prejudices, convictions,
attitudes, values, ways of thinking and acting, habits which
have become so much a part of us that it is agony even to
think of parting with them, and yet which are precisely what
prevent us from rightly interpreting the signs of the times,
from seeing life steadily and seeing it whole.*

Pedro Arrupe, S.J., *Justice with Faith Today*

By the fall of my second year, I was finally over the first-
year jitters and had stopped wondering if the Jesuits were
going to dismiss me for not closing the kitchen cabinets. After
my *secundi* brothers had taken their vows and went off to philosophy studies, Bill and I welcomed three new novices: Herman, a gregarious young man recently emigrated from Puerto
Rico, who had been working at Northeastern University;
David, a quiet, pious type who had worked as an architect in
Boston, and another David, a scholarly, owlish fellow who had
just graduated from Yale.

Over the past year, it had become evident that I was still
painfully unlettered in contemporary Catholicism, or at least
knew far less about the Church than the other novices. After all,
among my *secundi,* Michael was already a priest, George had
worked for the Jesuit Volunteer Corps, and the others seemed

to know all about the saints, the sacraments, and church history. At times it was embarrassing. When the *secundi* took vows in August, Jerry asked me to arrange the necessary items for the Mass.

"We'll need a corporal, two purificators, two patens, and a chalice," he said.

I stared at him stupidly, too embarrassed to say that, except for the chalice, I didn't know what any of those things were.

He remembered to whom he was speaking. "We need a placemat, two napkins, two saucers, and a cup."

As a result of my ignorance, but also to ensure that the other novices were up to speed as well, during conference that fall, one day a week was given over to reviewing books designed to introduce adults to Catholicism. I was amazed at how much things had changed since my C.C.D. classes. It helped me to see theology not as simply a memorization of dogma but as a way of helping adults live out their faith and make moral decisions.

One morning, for example, we were discussing the sacrament of reconciliation, formerly known as "penance" or "confession." When I last had heard about confesssion from Sister Mary Margaret in C.C.D., the stress was placed on our terrible mortal and venial sins. You had to say a good Act of Contrition ("O my God, I am heartily sorry for having offended thee . . . "), confess your sins with the proper intention, and say your penance before you could even begin to *think* about receiving Communion.

But the approach I read about in the novitiate was quite different: there was a greater emphasis on reconciliation with the community. Of course, sin was still around, as was confession and penance, but the stress was on God's forgiveness and God's desire for people to be reconciled with the rest of the community. In fact, it was now referred to as the "sacrament of reconciliation" instead of "penance" or "confession." This made a lot of sense, I thought.

"When did all this change?" I blurted out during conference.

"About twenty years ago," said a bemused David.

Which I calculated was about right: the last time I had ever studied Catholicism was at age ten.

For my fall ministry, I worked at St. Francis House, a homeless shelter run by the Franciscans and located in a poor part of downtown Boston. Homelessness was much in the news, and I wanted to meet the problem firsthand. The sister who organized the volunteers asked me to do a number of tasks: work in the kitchen, spend time in the "Day Room," where men and women congregated on cold winter days, and sort and distribute secondhand clothes in the basement.

I most enjoyed working in the kitchen, where we prepared meals for three and four hundred people daily. You spent a few hours cooking, an hour or so handing out the food, and another few hours cleaning the kitchen and the dining room after the guests had finished. It was easy work making, for example, fifty pounds of powdered mashed potatoes in steel trays, and it was certainly gratifying to ladle out food to a hungry person. There are few jobs where you see such immediate results.

Plus it was fun working with the volunteers in the kitchen—college students from the area, retired men and women, and professional people taking a day off to volunteer. (Who knew that there were so many people willing to take time out of their schedules to help? It certainly hadn't occurred to me to do anything like that before becoming a Jesuit.) We had a quick lunch after we had finished cooking—eating the same food that the guests would eat. Before the meals were served, we would stand in a circle, hold hands, and say grace.

One lesson I learned from the various novitiate ministries was how easy it was for me to stereotype. When I worked at Youville Hospital, I expected I would be working with The Sick, and in Jamaica with The Dying or The Poor. But this was not exactly accurate. I never worked with The Sick or The Dying and certainly not The Poor. In reality, I worked with Gladys and Gene and Duane and Ricaldo. Reducing people to a type was a signal disservice to them, effectively draining them of any individuality. Certainly it was important to understand things about

Jamaican culture, for example, or the dying process or the causes of homelessness to understand more fully these people and the context of lives. But you needed to go farther than that: you couldn't approach them simply as a sociological group— as individuals they were simply too different.

By the time I started working at St. Francis House, I figured I had already learned my lesson. But evidently I hadn't, since I ended up making the same mistake. I was working in the clothes room one winter morning, hunting around for a jacket for one of the men. The men and women told us their sizes and what kinds of clothes they needed, and the volunteers helped them select suitable clothing from the donated castoffs. I held up a short, orange corduroy jacket with a wide belt around the middle in the front and a large brass buckle.

"God, that's *ugly*," he said. "Do you think I would want to be seen in that?"

The guys around him laughed. "Yeah, that's *nasty!*" one said.

Initially, I thought, He's a Homeless Person, he should be *grateful!* But then I thought, Why should he want to wear something ugly just because he happens to be homeless? It doesn't mean that he's not an individual with feelings or taste or pride. I wouldn't want to wear it either!

I also discovered a tendency to romanticize the people with whom I worked and, at the same time, to overestimate my own contribution. The poor, dying person who would be overjoyed to see me and gratefully pour out her story of faith to me. Or the Jamaican boy tremendously thankful for my attention and who would, with my generous help, turn his life around. And how *thankful* the homeless would be for the food and clothing I was handing out! Thank you, Jim!

Now, sometimes this would happen—many of the people I worked with were, indeed, thankful. And said as much. And many came to be my friends and inspired me with their own goodness. On the other hand, sometimes it was just plain difficult to be around some of them. The Sick, The Dying, and The Homeless sometimes included the occasional Pain in the Ass.

"These mashed potatoes look lumpy," one of the guys in the long, crowded food line said as I handed him his tray. He was about the four-hundredth person I had served. He thrust back his tray. "Mash them again," he snapped.

"Give me a break," I said. "I have to eat them, too."

"Ha!" laughed another guy in line. And then to me: "You *tell* him kid!"

The fall continued—the novices prayed and worked and studied—without incident. Except one. In mid-November we received word from the New England provincial office that six Jesuits, along with their cook and her daughter, had been assassinated at the University of Central America in El Salvador, as a result of their work with the poor there.

It was strange: I felt a clear sense of loss as did the rest of the novitiate community, and the rest of the Society. It was odd to feel so close to people I had never met, especially the slain Jesuits. Yet I felt that these really were my brothers. It was as if someone in my family had died, and even my non-Jesuit friends recognized it. My friends and family called to say how sorry they were. At the same time, there was a definite, well, pride in the way that the Jesuits, along with the two women, had witnessed to their faith, by opting to remain with the poor in a dangerous place. Was this pride wrong? Maybe I was taking a perverse pride in the notoriety and fame it brought the Society of Jesus. The story was splashed on the front pages of every major newspaper.

But it wasn't that. Their actions spoke to something deeper in me. For while I had no desire to be a martyr (at least not yet), I hoped that I would someday have the same kind of faith—the faith that animates someone to work for God and God's people even to the point of death. These were, in Jesuit parlance, "men of the Exercises." "Men for others." And so we were proud of them and what they had stood for.

MOST OF THE second year revolved around the "Long Experiment," when the novices were sent to work full-time in a Jesuit ministry for four months. So in January, when our *primi* were sent off to Jamaica, Bill was sent to "our" high school in Maine and I to a small Jesuit-run school in New York City.

The Nativity Mission School is located in a former tenement building near Houston Street on the Lower East Side, with rooms that had been used by immigrants now serving as classrooms. That year the staff included one Jesuit priest, who served as headmaster, two Jesuit scholastics teaching as part of their regency, and five young lay volunteers, who were part of a program called the Jesuit Volunteer Corps, a national project for recent college graduates. A few of the volunteers lived in a tiny, cluttered apartment on the uppermost floor of the school. The dedicated Jesuit principal, whom the volunteers and students called Father Jack, lived in a tiny room, a closet really, off of one of the classrooms.

I lived at the Jesuit parish on Second Avenue, also called Nativity, a few blocks away from the school. The community included the two Jesuit regents, three priests who worked in the parish, and one who worked as a chaplain in a hospital uptown. We saw little of the chaplain, since he spent most of his time in the hospital and often slept there overnight. Unlike the novitiate, I had no problems with "poverty" here. The residence was a bit run-down, especially the kitchen in the basement, which was situated next to a parish meeting hall. And in some spots the house was in urgent need of repair: drafty windows, broken furniture, missing ceiling tiles, that sort of thing. The novitiate was starting to look better and better.

Most of the boys at Nativity came from recently immigrated Dominican and Puerto Rican families, and had parents who often barely spoke English. The fifty or so boys got a great deal of attention and love from the small staff at the school.

And the teachers worked tremendously hard; their schedules were crushing, their energy astonishing. Classes began at 8:00 in the morning and continued through lunch. Since there was only a postage-stamp sized kitchen at the school, Fr. Jack purchased lunches for the children from a high school run by the Christian Brothers three blocks away. Every day a few Nativity boys would stack forty school lunches in an ancient shopping cart at La Salle High School and wheel them down Second Avenue and across Houston Street to Nativity. Food was frequently dropped on the sidewalk *en route.* I could tell, for example, that the boys would be having turkey when, on my walk to the school, I spied a dollop of cranberry sauce sitting forlornly on the pavement. The teachers, on the other hand, were fed by the mothers and *abuelitas* of the parish, who prepared fragrant pots of *arroz con pollo* and *arroz con tuna* for us. After lunch came a brief recess and the kids returned to classes, which ended at 3:00. Since many of the boys came from broken homes or homes where there were few places to study, they remained at Nativity until dinner time. At 5:00, the school was locked up, and all of us went home for dinner.

Most of the teachers went to the daily 5:15 Mass at the parish, celebrated in the small Jesuit community chapel. In other words, the daily community Mass, which in most communities was reserved exclusively for Jesuits, here included teachers and parishioners from the Lower East Side. There were three or four regular parishioners at the 5:15 Mass—all elderly, poor women. One of them prayed every day for "the sick, the poor, and the suffering." Another always prayed for "my son, Alexander, the priest." The third woman said nothing. This fusion of the Jesuit community, Nativity teachers, and the elderly parishioners provided for some quintessentially Catholic moments.

After a gospel passage on Jesus' teaching in the synagogue ("Is this not the carpenter's son?") Father Jack offered a brief homily about the Jewishness of Jesus. "Jesus was born and raised a Jew in a Jewish family," he noted.

Two of the women found this difficult to swallow.

"But of course," said one, "Jesus *was* a Christian."

"No," said Father Jack, patiently. "He was a Jew. He was raised as one and died as one."

"But he *stopped* being Jewish when he founded Christianity," said another woman. "Right?"

"Not really."

"He couldn't have been Jewish! He was *Jesus!*" said the first woman insistently.

I didn't want to leave Father Jack out in the theological cold, so I jumped in. "You know," I said, "I read somewhere that if Jesus were to return to earth today, he's probably feel more at home in a synagogue than in a temple, because of his Jewishness."

"Well," one of the women sighed with resignation. "I guess it's just one of those mysteries."

After Mass and dinner, the students and teachers would return to Nativity for the study hall. While the amount of time the students spent in school seemed excessive at first, it quickly became obvious to me that this was one of the keys to the school's success. The kids benefited greatly from the caring supervision and attention from the staff. It was a safe environment and, more often than not, the surroundings were much more conducive to study than their homes were.

The day ended at 10:00 P.M., when one of the teachers drove the kids home in Nativity's van—since the neighborhood was somewhat dangerous.

When I was "missioned" to Nativity, my novice director said that I probably wouldn't be able to follow a regular teacher's schedule of 8:00 A.M. to 10:00 P.M. We both realized that the schedule would leave little time for prayer and reflection. So I went to Nativity as a sort of adjunct teacher, working "only" from noon until 10:00 at night. As a result, my job was almost wholly unstructured. Father Jack first asked me to develop an after-school program for the Nativity graduates who were now in high school, teach a few courses and, more or less, pitch in. This was what we referred to at GE as a "special project." And at GE, I used to warn employees assiduously to avoid special projects—they were generally unstructured and, as a result, left people confused about their exact responsibilities. And, indeed, I soon felt frustrated with an unstructured job with no clear parameters. Part of me was also embarrassed that I wasn't a full-fledged teacher. On the other hand, I soon realized that much of the work that everyone else did was unstructured as well, so I wasn't completely bereft.

The first thing I did with the Nativity "graduates" now in high school was to organize evening talks where some professionals could discuss their jobs. I thought it might help give the kids an idea of what kind of opportunities were on the other side of high school, since some of their parents were underemployed. I solicited some friends to do this, figuring it would be an education for them, too. And I tried to feature Hispanic professionals, since I thought they might be more effective role models. Sometimes, though, it backfired.

One night I invited a Hispanic architect to speak. After a stupefyingly dull presentation, he asked if there were any questions. One of the boys roused himself from his stupor to ask, "Yeah, what are you doing now? I mean are you on a project or something?"

"Yes, I'm redesigning the bathrooms at City Hall."

"Yeah, *that* sounds like fun!" said one.

The boys burst into laughter. I knew that I had seriously reduced the possibility of a future architect coming from the group.

I also organized some short day trips for the high school students. One day we went uptown for a tour of the NBC studios. I still knew some people whom I had placed there when I worked for GE, which had purchased NBC in 1986. My friends were able to arrange a tour for the students, and were willing to speak to them about what it was like to work there. Some of these sixteen- and seventeen-year-old boys, who had spent their entire lives in New York City, had, I discovered, never ventured further north than 14th Street. I was surprised at how they reacted as we came out of the subway, looking up at the tall buildings at Rockefeller Center much as any first-time tourist in New York would. "Wow, Mr. Martin," said one of them inside the NBC building, "I never seen wall-to-wall carpeting."

Leading around fifteen high school kids was a decided challenge. During the tour they cheerfully ignored the guide's instructions, peeking into empty offices and wandering down halls that were not on the tour. The tour guide, an attractive young woman, had an even harder time than I did.

"This is where *The Today Show* is filmed," she said cheerily as we stepped into one of the studios.

"The *what* show? I never seen that," said one boy. "When's it on?"

"Every morning at seven!" she said.

"Shee-it," he said.

"Well," she said, recovering. "Does anyone have any questions?"

"Yeah. How much money do you make?"

I'm not sure if she even stammered out a response before the inevitable next question.

"Yeah," one boy said smiling slyly. "I gotta question. You wanna go *out* some time?"

Each afternoon I tutored some of the younger students. Angel and Jimmy were both ten-year-olds who were having trouble reading. So I hunted down some good children's book to make it more enjoyable for them.

Jimmy liked *Encyclopedia Brown*, the famous boy detective. He said that once he got past the first word of the title it wasn't such a hard book at all. Angel picked out one of my favorite childhood books, *Island of the Blue Dolphins*, which he enjoyed even though its protagonist was a *girl*. The rest of my time was filled teaching a painting class in the afternoons and monitoring study hall in the afternoons and evenings, where I answered questions about homework and helped the students with spelling and math. But there was a disciplinary side of the job—keeping the room quiet—which proved daunting. It was difficult not to laugh at the occasional jokes and pranks. The students also asked me endless questions, which provided the boys with their only valid excuse to talk.

"Mr. Martin," one of the students, named Bobby, asked me one day, "Were you really making a lot of money before you were a Jesuit?"

"Yeah, I guess so," I said.

"Did you, like, have your own apartment?"

"Uh-huh."

"A car?" he continued.

"Yup."

"And now you're doing *this?* Man, why'd you give it up?"

"Because I like this better than anything I've done before."

Much eye rolling from Bobby. "Man, you're *crazy!*"

But it was the truth. Even though I was just doing small things, like monitoring study halls, substituting for the occasional class, and running an afternoon art class, I felt infinitely more satisfied than I had in any of my jobs at GE. At a point in life when I expected to have a secure job, a good salary, a well-appointed house, and a car (or two), I had instead none of those things, and it didn't seem to matter at all.

ONE EVENING in the kitchen in the Jesuit community, I was talking to our cook, Aura. She prepared fantastic Dominican dishes, many of them including fried food. Consequently, there was a tiny spot of oil on the floor, which I slipped on; I felt my foot twist under me and heard something snap. I limped back to study hall at school.

The next morning, my foot had grown so swollen that I could barely walk. I limped to a nearby hospital, where an emergency room doctor told me I had broken a tiny bone. As I watched, incredulous, he cut the leg of my jeans and began to bandage my foot, winding yards of slimy wet gauze up to my knee. I walked back to the school on crutches with a huge cast.

"Mr. *Martin!*" the kids yelled as I walked through the door.

"What happened?" Twenty students ran up to ask what kind of accident I had been in. They also begged to use my crutches. So at lunchtime, while I sat eating with the other teachers, the kids played around on the crutches. "I hope I break *my* leg!" said one.

Michelle, one of the volunteer teachers, asked her classes to pray that Mr. Martin's foot would get better.

The next morning, I stepped gingerly into the shower. At the doctor's instruction, I had wrapped a plastic garbage bag over the cast to keep it dry. But to no avail. The cast immediately became soaked with water; it felt like it weighed fifty pounds. I returned to the hospital where another doctor, after taking a few X-rays, told me that I certainly did not need such a big cast. I would, he told me, have to be on crutches for only a few weeks. He swiftly cut it off and gave me a nice Ace bandage instead, which covered only my ankle.

I walked back into school.

"Mr. *Martin!*" the kids came running up to me. "Your leg's better! We prayed for you in class and now your leg is better! It's, like, a *miracle!*"

IT WAS FUN living in Manhattan again, albeit on a much slimmer budget than when I had worked with GE. At the time, I was given a stipend of seventy dollars. This was an increase over the previous year's "salary" of thirty-five dollars, which prompted my old roommate Rob to say that I must be doing well, since I had received a one-hundred percent raise.

Many of my college friends worked in Manhattan, and most of my GE friends still lived nearby. A number of them were still uncomfortable with the "whole Jesuit thing," as one friend referred to it. It shouldn't have surprised me, since I had jumped into the Society of Jesus so unexpectedly. Perhaps I would have felt the same way if one of them had done something similar. A few were still worried that I was doing something willfully stupid. And why wouldn't they be? They knew very little about the Jesuits.

Some, like Rob, were tremendously supportive, even to the point of asking me about Jesuit traditions, spirituality, and prayer. And my few friends who were religious were, not surprisingly, extremely supportive. Jacque, my born-again Christian friend from Penn, never tired of hearing about the work I was doing, the prayer, the retreats, my plans for the future.

But most were still wary about the Society of Jesus and religious life in general. This was obvious from our conversations. And they were *particularly* uncomfortable about discussing prayer and faith. This I called the "squirm factor." If I talked about the novitiate, other Jesuits, the type of work I was doing, Jesuit formation—that was fine, more or less. But if I inadvertently mentioned something like prayer or contemplation—or God forbid, God—they grew increasingly uncomfortable and began squirming in their seats. Typically, they would labor to change the topic.

But even those suspicious of religion were warmer to the whole "good works" aspect. Jamaica, Nativity, working with the homeless—these things appealed to them. And happily, if they felt comfortable with the work I did, they often grew increasingly interested in the spiritual foundations for the work. Still, it was odd dancing around my faith, which had become an important part of my life and one that I freely discussed with my Jesuit brothers. That some of my other friends weren't ready to hear about it rendered much of my life incommunicable.

Only a very few friends seemed actively to dislike the Jesuits, and I felt uncomfortable around them. None of them came out and said I was "wrong," but a few drew me into heated debates about the record of the Catholic Church, its "wealth," as well as its record on women's rights, birth control, abortion, etc. The existence of God and the reality of prayer were figments of my imagination, they suggested. The Jesuits struck them as distinctly cultish. I knew that they appreciated the good works, but the fact that it had anything to do with the Catholic Church made even working with the poor suspect. The Jesuits must have an ulterior motive for that kind of work. "What was their *political* motivation?" asked one GE friend suspiciously. How did the Jesuits *really* use the money that people donated? The Church sure had a lot of real estate, didn't it? They lamented my having joined the Jesuits. And I lamented their mindset.

Bruce told me that one college friend, at a New Year's Eve party, had sighed heavily and said, "It's just too bad about Jim. He used to enjoy doing so many different things, like going to museums and movies and things. Now he's probably never going to be able to do any of that."

"He's joined the Jesuits," Bruce retorted. "He's not dead."

Certainly I didn't want to lose friends because of the Jesuits. I hoped that once they got to know the Jesuits better they would be more comfortable about my decision. And, indeed, as they spent time around other Jesuits and around me, most could see that I wasn't becoming some brainwashed automaton. Still, I was uncomfortable around the few who were hostile, and began to gravitate away from them. (That, in turn, made me feel guilty.) But it was difficult enough being a novice without having to spend time around people berating me about my choice.

During my time at Nativity, I also got a taste of what it was like to be a public "religious figure." While I was still on crutches, the staff were invited to a benefit for the school hosted by a sort of young executives' charity organization in Manhattan. In May, they sponsored a dinner-dance in a large club on the West Side. It was a humid night, and I sweated just thinking about traipsing around on crutches in a jacket and tie. Better to wear a clerical shirt—it was short-sleeved and could still pass for being "dressed up." Plus, I was curious to see what it would be like.

"Ooooh. Hello, *Father!*" the teachers said in unison as I emerged from the rectory. We took a cab to the club, out of deference to my crutches.

The hall was crowded with young executive types not unlike, well . . . *me* two years ago. The teachers and I settled down to our table for dinner, which was served by some Nativity graduates who were being paid handsomely for the evening. "Hey, Mr. Martin, you're a priest!" they said upon spotting the collar.

It was difficult to circulate on crutches, so I parked myself by our table and let my friends bring me drinks. One well-dressed partygoer bumped into me on his way to the bar. "Watch it!" he snapped as he made his way past.

He saw my collar when he had passed. "Oh, *Father*, I'm sorry!" he said, suddenly full of contrition. "I didn't see you there at all. I'm really *sorry!*"

One corporate type approached me to say what great work we were doing at Nativity. He was very chatty and asked some intelligent questions about the school. I asked him what he did for a living.

"Well, Father, I work in finance. For an investment bank." He paused, perhaps thinking that he had already lost me. "Now, an investment bank sort of handles other people's money and helps them to invest it. That's different from a *commercial* bank."

"Uh-huh. I remember the difference," I said, thinking back to my interview with Salomon Brothers. "Actually I used to be in finance myself. I worked for GE Capital." He stared at me, astonished, and his jaw actually dropped open. I had never seen anyone's jaw drop, I remember thinking. I might as well have said, "I can fly, too!" After a few uncomfortable words, he made his way back to the drink table.

At the end of the night, a very drunk, very attractive woman approached me. After some desultory small talk, she grabbed my arm and drew close. "You know what I really need tonight, Father?"

I didn't.

"Someone to sleep with." She looked at me pointedly.

I didn't know what to say, so I said nothing.

"Can I ask you something . . . if it's not too personal?"

"I guess so," I said hesitantly.

"Are you an alcoholic?"

"Uh, no." I was drinking ginger ale at the time.

"Are you gay?" she asked.

"What?"

"Are you gay, Father?"

"I thought you said this wasn't going to be personal," I said.

"You're straight, aren't you?" she said. "I can tell."

I gently removed her hand from my arm and said thanks for coming.

She staggered off. One of the Nativity boys, Miguel, came up to me and said, "Hey, Mr. Martin, who was *that?*"

"Listen, Miguel," I said. "if you ever want to attract women just buy a black shirt like this one."

"No kidding! Where can I buy them?"

I never grew totally comfortable with my scattered job at Nativity. Perhaps I was still too used to the structure I had at GE. But, if anything, Nativity seemed to benefit from the unstructured environment. Things were accomplished despite the craziness (or maybe *because* of it), and the kids felt loved and at home, which perhaps they would not have in a more spartan, regimented school. Yet, despite any frustrations about the job, I loved the kids and admired the staff and the school's mission. It was just where a Jesuit should be. On my last day, we had a special going-away cake at the school lunch. After Fr. Jack made a little speech, the kids banged on the tables and stamped on the floor and hollered in appreciation. It was better than any paycheck I'd ever received.

ALL OF THE novices returned to Arrupe House from their experiments in early June. The summer *ordo* was relaxed: we studied Spanish in Cambridge (except for Spanish-speaking Herman, who studied English) and did plenty of yard work. Then a week of vacation (or "villa") with my family and one week with the other novices on Cape Cod.

For the *secundi*, it was also time to start thinking more seriously about vows, which were scheduled in August. I never doubted that I wanted to take vows. But now, after two years of discernment, it was time to make formal "application" to my superiors. Actually, I was told initially that I had been approved for something else. "Congratulations," said the novice director one day in June. "You've been approved to apply for vows."

I hadn't realized that this was even a step in the process— being approved to *apply.* "I thought you just applied," I said.

"Oh no, you have to be approved first," said Jerry. "*Then* you apply."

"Oh, thanks," I said. "I guess."

The novice director asked Bill and me to reflect on our experience as novices in the past two years. And we were to write *informatios* about each other and, I was surprised to learn, ourselves. But writing your own *informatio* was a useful exercise in self-evaluation. (At the very least it was a challenge to answer questions like "Would you like to live with this man in community?" and "How well do you feel you know this Jesuit?") Finally, we were expected to make a three-day "vow retreat" before Vow Day. All of this was an opportunity to reflect on Jesuit life—which of our experiences confirmed our vocations and which did not, what we were comfortable with and what we weren't, what we liked and what we didn't. In other words, were we meant to be Jesuits? First, of course, I had to think about the vows.

Poverty hadn't presented much of a problem for me as a novice. Though I had earned a good salary at GE, the money itself had never been a big deal. My only extravagances had been a few short vacations in Europe. Other than that, I socked all my money away. So I thought that giving it up would be easy.

And part of it *was* easy. No checking account, no credit cards, no car payments, no rent, no worrying about which job would lead to making the most money, no wondering if your salary was as high as it should be or as high as the next person's. Ridding myself of those worries was wonderfully freeing, as it was meant to be. Overall, living simply seemed to suit me fine.

But there are real sacrifices on a budget of seventy dollars a month. Often it seemed that my monthly budget was consumed entirely by toiletries and long-distance phone calls. (I started shaving every other day just to save on shaving cream.) And I was totally dependent on the Jesuits for my financial needs. *De jure*, I owned nothing. *De facto* (as well as *de jure*, come to think of it) I had precious little money to "do" things. Anything I needed or wanted I had to ask for, and I had to be prepared that the answer might be no.

Jesuit work also took me to places where luxurious living was either impossible or scandalous to the people with whom we worked. A homeless shelter in Boston. A Kingston slum. The Lower East Side of New York. It is difficult to feel you deserve or even *need* many things in the face of the standard of living around you. I couldn't return to my Jesuit community in

Kingston after having worked with boys who literally had nothing, and complain about the food. Or rather if I did, I felt a pang of guilt.

Still, as a novice, I occasionally found it difficult to reconcile what I understood as "poverty" and the way that we sometimes lived it. I still clung to a perhaps overly legalistic notion of poverty as absolute. But while "ours" is certainly a poverty of simplicity and detachment, of using only what we needed, it is not a poverty of utter destitution, as Ignatius had pointed out. Ignatius knew from his own experience the problems that came with taking poverty to the extreme—no food means no health means no ministry. That I understood. We needed some things in order to do our work.

But I sometimes wondered how we could justify "needing" so many things. A few years after novitiate, I visited a Jesuit community where breakfasts were cooked to order every morning. And another large community where every Jesuit had his own car. Sometimes I found it confusing. Sometimes, when I was feeling particularly superior, I could be judgmental. But sometimes, when I remembered that I myself was far from perfect, and that it was wrong to judge any of my brother Jesuits, who try to live poverty honestly and sincerely, I could relax about it all.

Occasionally, I could even see the humor in all of our imperfections.

"If this is poverty," one Jesuit whispered at a lavish meal in a Jesuit community, "bring on chastity!"

And despite my exacting standards and tendency to judge others, I realized that I couldn't live in grinding poverty. One night in Kingston, our little group of scholastics had dinner with a group of Canadian Jesuits living in a neighborhood slum. Of course, I was living in a slum as well. The difference was that they were living in a tiny home similar to those of the people around them, with limited physical space, poor plumbing, and only intermittent electricity. On the other hand, I was living in a large, secure compound surrounded by barbed wire, with more than occasional hot water and someone to cook my meals to boot. Their manner of living, I thought, was more authentic, and

I was strongly attracted to it. But I knew I couldn't live that way—at least not yet.

There is also a deeper type of poverty that a Jesuit faces as well—a spiritual poverty that everyone faces at some point. The poverty of being simply human, prone to failure, to sickness, to hunger, to disappointment. The inability to heal people or "do" something at Youville hospital, the knowledge that no matter how many hours I spent tutoring in Kingston, the Alpha boys were probably destined to a life of poverty. The understanding that the same men and women I met at the St. Francis homeless shelter would probably remain homeless. And knowing that no matter how much time we spent with the boys at Nativity, some of the boys would undoubtedly face lives of struggle and hardship. Without faith, I think, this type of realization can lead to despair. It is this type of poverty that forces you to rely on God.

But the years in the novitiate helped me to see that accepting these poverties can be profoundly freeing. Accepting that everything comes from God frees you from the myth of self-reliance and independence. Ultimately, you give up trying to solve everyone's problems on your own. Not ameliorate, but solve. As long as you rely simply on yourself, you are doomed to despair. But surrendering yourself to spiritual poverty—the poverty of your own limitations—frees you from this despair and makes your ministry more fruitful by allowing God to work through you more effectively. In short, you move from despair to hope.

The second vow—chastity—was always more difficult. Sex is great. It is certainly a challenge to abstain from sex, and from physical intimacy. But more difficult than the lack of physical intimacy is not having one person to whom you can turn for support. The "exclusive relationship," as its known in religious parlance. Sometimes I felt a twinge of envy and regret when I saw two people walking arm in arm, knowing that my life did not include that.

But there is freedom here, too. A Jesuit friend once told me, "I couldn't marry just one person—I've fallen in love so many times with so many people, I'd have to marry hundreds of people." That's not exactly the way I look at it, but he was expressing the fundamental goal of chastity—which, of course, is love. And even chastity does not preclude one from falling in love. I've fallen in love plenty times since becoming a Jesuit. It's natural and, as David was constantly reminding me in spiritual direction, if you *didn't* fall in love there would probably be something wrong with you. Falling in love and being in love are both gifts from God. It's a question of what you *do* when you fall in love as a celibate. Do you deny or repress the feelings and become twisted and frustrated, or do you try to integrate them into your chaste life?

A chaste person tries, like Jesus did, to love as many people as possible. Some cynics say that loving everyone means you love no one. And I suppose that sometimes this is one danger of the celibate life. In a Peanuts comic strip, Charlie Brown says to Linus that he could never become a doctor because Linus didn't love mankind. "I love mankind," says Linus, "It's people I can't stand!"

On a practical level, though, I know that I have more energy and time for others when I am living chastely—to pay attention, to listen, to be intimate—than I would if I were in an exclusive relationship. This doesn't mean that chastity is meant for everyone, or that it's somehow "better" than being single or being married. It's not. Chastity is simply another way of loving that works for some people. Like married people, I don't always live out my vows perfectly and, sometimes, I make a complete mess of things. But when it works, it's wonderful. It's liberating and enables me to experience God's love and grace.

Obedience always seemed, at least as a novice, to be the easiest of the three vows. After all, I used to take orders in GE and never thought twice about it. It amazes me that some people who are willing to work fifteen-hour days and uproot themselves and their families to move across the country for a corporation can't understand how anyone could take a vow of obedience. "How can you let someone tell you what to *do?*" As if a law firm or bank or university doesn't do exactly the same thing—and often with far less input.

Joe, the spiritual director who lived at the novitiate, told me that every year on July 31, the provincial's *status* would be released, which announced the Jesuit assignments for the next year. One year, after Joe had finished his philosophy studies—this must have been in the late 1950s—the annual *status* was posted and listed him as teaching chemistry at the Cranwell School, one of the old Jesuit prep schools in western Massachusetts.

"I went to the provincial," he told me, "thinking there must have been a mistake. Not only had I never taught chemistry, I had never even studied it in school!

"But the provincial told me that there was no mistake," said Joe. "They needed a chemistry teacher."

"So what did you do?" I asked, astonished.

"Ha!" he laughed. "I taught chemistry for three years! And you know what? I got pretty good at it, too!"

This type of obedience also means that Jesuits must shift from job to job over their careers, depending on the needs of the Society and, more broadly, the Church. Saint Ignatius, attuned to the pride that often attended positions of authority, also directed that Jesuit provincials and superiors hold those positions only for a limited time. After that, these men returned to living with the brothers who had formerly been their subjects. It keeps Jesuits grounded and made it (more) difficult to get a swelled head. Ignatius also stipulated that, as far as possible, Jesuits resist being made bishops or cardinals. In fact, imbedded in the final vow formula for Jesuits who have completed their formation is a promise not to seek high office in the Society of Jesus.

But for every Jesuit who has held a dozen different jobs in his career and has bounced around like a ping-pong ball from community to community, there is another Jesuit who has stayed planted resolutely in one place and in one ministry. (And woe betide the provincial who tries to move him.) "I've been in this room for forty years," an older Jesuit once said to me. I didn't know whether to commiserate or congratulate.

More recently, obedience reflects the kind of decision making that St. Ignatius favored, where the desires of both the Jesuit and his superior are seen as important. (Which is not to say that Ignatius wasn't big on obedience. He wrote in the *Constitutions* that a Jesuit should be willing to listen to a request from his superior "as if it were coming from Christ.") So it's not usually a question of being dragged off kicking and screaming to teach chemistry somewhere. Often, an equally difficult obedience is the simple obedience of daily work, of being true to what you are sent to do, whether it's teaching, working, studying, or praying *pro Soc. et Eccles.*, and realizing that, although you might find it hard to believe, this is God's will for you. Or at least as near to God's will as you and your superiors are able to discern. Ultimately, a Jesuit believes that through prayer and conversation between you and your superior, God's will can be accomplished.

When I was at Nativity School and wondering whether my job was as important as the people who taught full time, I had to remind myself that I was there under obedience. When I was bored or felt useless at Youville, I had to remind myself about obedience. When I wanted somehow to avoid washing the old men in Kingston (which was every day), obedience certainly wasn't the only thing that kept me there, but it certainly helped to keep me from entertaining thoughts about quitting. Daily obedience. And, looking back, I was happy I stayed in each case.

AS WE MOVED towards vows, the novice director also asked us to reflect on our own "prayer life," that is, the way we pray and the role of prayer in our daily lives.

It was amazing to realize that, in just two years, prayer had become a central element of my life, almost as regular as breathing. If for one day I didn't pray, I felt off-center, out of touch with the deepest part of myself—the bond that tied me to God. And by the end of my *secundi* year, after two years of daily prayer, weekly spiritual direction, and plenty of time on retreat, I had also come to know what types of things helped me to pray. I knew, for one thing, that I needed real quiet to pray—

quiet on both the outside and the inside. And since external quiet was often difficult to find in the novitiate, I usually prayed in the house chapel (the quietest place in the house) in the late mornings, after conference (the quietest time in the house).

A Jesuit friend told me that he had once traveled to a Trappist monastery on retreat, looking forward to his time of quiet contemplation. Like most monasteries that support themselves, this one had a special business—baking bread. My friend imagined himself working with the jolly monks, pulling out newly baked loaves from warm brick ovens, the aroma of fresh bread hanging in the air as they softly chanted their daily prayers. But soon after his arrival, my friend found himself working in a huge, noisy bread factory. When the time came for prayers, the monks simply took their breviaries to one corner of the factory and shouted their prayers over the tremendous din of the machines!

But more important than learning about the wheres and whens of prayer was learning about the hows, and for this I relied primarily on insights and advice from the novice director and my spiritual director.

Another helpful insight into prayer came from a terrific little book called *God and You*, written by a Jesuit named William Barry, an experienced spiritual director. In his book, he suggests that a relationship with God can be fruitfully compared to a relationship with another person. Obviously, it's not *exactly* the same: after all, most of our friends have not created the universe *ex nihilo*. Rather, the point of the book is that the way you think about personal relationships can help you think about, and deepen, your relationship with God. For example, being in a good relationship means that you need to spend time with the other person. As in your relationship with God. And in any relationship you naturally want to learn as much as you can about the other person: her life story, her struggles, her joys. The same is true in your relationship with God—and here is where Scripture comes in handy. (If you want to get to know Jesus, get to know the Gospels.) Similarly, any good friendship requires one to listen to the other. You would scarcely consider yourself a good friend if all you did was talk and ask for things. (As we often do in prayer!) Listening is just as important in any relationship, perhaps most important.

Thinking about God in this way—in terms of a personal relationship—made the ups and downs of prayer seem much less frightening. At the beginning of a relationship, for example, there's often a period of "infatuation"; all you want is to spend time with the other person. As it is with prayer: when you begin to pray, all you want is to spend time with God, so enjoyable is it. But the relationship needs to move beyond that superficial level and into something deeper. Like any friendship, it needs to grow and be open to change. And so prayer changes throughout your life: sometimes it will come naturally, almost easily, and feel rich and deep; at other times, prayer will be exceedingly difficult, almost a chore, and yield precious little in the way of "results." But the important thing is—again, as in any friendship—to keep at it and, ultimately, to come to know and love the other person more deeply. As the Jesuit theologian Karl Rahner wrote, the important thing is not knowing *about* God, it's knowing God.

Part of prayer is also the basic trust that for those who seek God sincerely, God will eventually come. As one Islamic saying has it, for every step you take towards God, God takes two steps towards you; and if you come to God walking, God comes to you running.

For me, prayer in the novitiate was mostly on an emotional level—a feeling of love or gratitude or awe in response to how God was at work in my life. And over the course of the two years, I came to know God—and myself—better. That's pretty simplistic, I know, but then again, I'm not Ignatius of Loyola, Thérèse of Lisieux, or even Thomas Merton. It was difficult enough just to be myself.

As AUGUST approached, Bill and I spent more time preparing for Vow Day. First we wrote out, in longhand, four separate vow "formulas" in a bound book that was kept in the novitiate. The first was the official vow formula that we would pronounce during the Mass, the same formula that Jesuits have used for centuries. I flipped through the latest book, which went back about ten years, looking at the handwriting of the novices who had precede me: some bold, some crabbed, some illegible, but all making the same promises to God. And we wrote our promises to accept whatever "grade" or status the Society gave to us. We would sign each of the vow formulas immediately after the Mass.

We were also asked to decide if we wanted to take a "vow name," sort of like a confirmation name one might take. I figured: Hey, a free name, why not? During our three-day vow retreat, I realized (among other things) that Jesus loved me even though I was very imperfect—like St. Peter, I thought. So I asked to take Peter for my vow name.

After the New England provincial approved us for vows, we scheduled a Mass in the Church of the Immaculate Conception, the chapel attached to the New England province offices. It is a beautiful church that had been renovated just a few years before, with a high, vaulted ceiling punctuated with busts of Jesuit saints atop tall, white pillars. High above the ornate stone altar is an elaborate mural of Mary among the saints in heaven. However, beautifully renovated though it was, the church was still not air conditioned. Vow Day was August 18, so we were concerned about the heat. In any event, we concluded, there would be fans in the church so it couldn't be all that bad.

Preparing for vows was almost like preparing for a wedding. Printing the invitations and programs, selecting the songs, the readings, the homilist, the celebrants, and even finding a caterer to provide food for the guests after the ceremony. (That $250 we had donated to the novitiate on entrance day was finally put to use.) The mounting expenses put me in mind of a tale about Pedro Arrupe, the former Jesuit superior general. One of the provincials was explaining to Fr. Arrupe how his novitiate needed to be moved from a wealthy neighborhood to a poorer one. This would entail finding a new house and fixing it up, which would be quite expensive. "Ah," said Father Arrupe, "it costs a lot of money to keep our men poor, doesn't it?"

August 18 was a sunny, sultry day; I was already sweating as I left the novitiate with the other novices at 12:00 for the church.

After ensuring that everything was in place for the Mass—the programs, the flowers, the organist—I wandered through the church and greeted everyone. Happily, my parents by this point had reconciled and gotten back together and my sister was engaged, so my family was not only back to its former size, but had grown. My relatives and friends from high school had driven up from Philadelphia, and friends from Penn flew in from all over the East Coast, and coworkers from GE came in from New York and Stamford. The teachers from Nativity crammed into the school van and made the pilgrimage from New York. Some of my sister's friends from Harvard were even planning on coming. Bruce and his mother drove all the way from Washington, D.C. "To her it's almost as good as *me* being a Jesuit," he told me a few weeks before Vow Day.

The organ music started and I dashed to the rear of the church to take my place at the end of a long line of priests who were already walking up the center aisle. As I was collecting my thoughts, my sister's college friends arrived and, spying me, joined the procession and started chatting. Hi, how are you? You look good. So do you. Thanks for coming.

Gradually, I started up the aisle.

"So, when does the Mass start?" said one, as she walked beside me.

"Um, now, actually," I said. "You're in the processional. Maybe you should find a seat."

The Mass proceeded smoothly. My sister and Bill's sister each read passages from Scripture. For the Gospel Reading, Bill and I had selected the passage from John 21, where Jesus says to the disciples, "Feed my sheep." We took that to be a good description of service in the Church.

After David's homily, he and Jerry began the Eucharistic Prayer. There were a number of priests concelebrating the liturgy, who stood beside the altar as the presider spoke the prayers of the Mass. Presently, I noticed that one of them, a

Jesuit named Dan, who had worked with Bill in his Long Experiment, was looking distinctly unwell. He had turned a strange, pallid color. That's interesting, I thought; I had only read about people looking grey but had never seen it. Suddenly, Dan sat down in his chair with a plop. A few of the other priests bent over to ask if he was all right. It was by then enormously hot in the church. Then he fainted and slumped over in the chair.

Since there were a few Jesuit physicians in the church, two of them raced up the aisle to help Dan. As we watched in horror, they laid him on the carpeted floor of the church and started fanning him. Later, I would learn that Dan was on a liquid diet and hadn't really eaten anything at all that day. The combination of the diet and the stifling heat had simply overwhelmed him. Anyway, here was this poor Jesuit lying on the floor during a vow Mass with two priests around him, and the rest of the province looking on. He looked understandably mortified.

One of the Jesuit physicians, a good friend named Myles, caught my eye as he knelt down to take Dan's pulse. At this point, I was probably as grey as the priest in question. Over his shoulder, Myles smiled and silently mouthed one word to me: "Congratulations!"

Jerry was now in the middle of the Eucharistic Prayer and about to say the words of consecration. He later explained that he felt that stopping the Mass would only direct more attention on Dan and further embarrass him, so he decided to continue.

Jerry approached me after the Consecration. "We'll have to do your vows later," he whispered.

What? Horrified, I thought he meant another *day*. Actually, he only meant a little later in the ceremony. Normally, Jesuits pronounce their vows after the Consecration, as the novice director holds the host before them. But since at that point there was still a supine body on the floor, he decided it might be more prudent to wait until after Communion.

As Jerry and David began distributing Communion we heard the distant wail of sirens. A few minutes later, an emergency medical team burst into the church, wheeled a squeaking gurney directly up the front aisle and, after giving Dan some water, loaded him on the gurney and processed out the church under the watchful eyes of the congregation. It was the dramatic high point of the Mass. From then on, everything else would be anti-climactic.

It was, of course, not exactly the ceremony I had planned.

After Communion had been distributed, Jerry motioned that I should now pronounce my vows. So, while the audience looked on, sweating, I knelt down on the surprisingly cool carpet. I closed my eyes, asked God to be with me, and started speaking:

> Almighty and eternal God, I, James Peter Martin, understand how unworthy I am in Your divine sight. Yet I am strengthened by Your infinite compassion and mercy, and am moved by the desire to serve You. I vow to Your Divine Majesty, before the most Holy Virgin Mary and the entire heavenly court, perpetual chastity, poverty, and obedience in the Society of Jesus. I promise that I will enter this same Society to spend my life in it forever. I understand all of these things according to the Constitutions of the Society of Jesus. Therefore, by Your boundless goodness and mercy, and through the blood of Jesus Christ, I humbly ask that You judge this total commitment of myself acceptable, and as You have freely given me the desire to make this offering, so may You also give me the abundant grace to fulfill it.

Pronouncing vows was a terrific feeling. Even in the midst of all the craziness—the preparations, the nervousness, the guests, the heat, the fainting, the EMS team—I was wonderfully concentrated. It was like praying out loud to God in front of my friends and family. And I thought, yes, this is where I should be; this is where I belong. This is seeing life whole.

After the liturgy, I was surrounded by dozens of priests in white albs who threw their arms around me in congratulations. Of course, Dan's fainting was the main topic of conversation. "Well, no one will ever forget *your* vow ceremony!" said the provincial. I made a mental note to get ordained a priest in the winter. And to make sure there was plenty of water.

After Bill and I had signed all the official documents in the church sacristy, we drove back for a reception in the backyard at Arrupe House. I was relieved to shed my suit, climb into some shorts and a T-shirt, and spend time with friends. I was delighted that so many of my friends and family, who had been doubtful about my entering, could see that I was happy.

"Hello, *Father*," George, my old friend from Penn, said to me.

"I'm not a father yet." I corrected him. "That doesn't come for another nine or ten years."

He looked distraught. "You're kidding. I have to come up for *another* ceremony?"

That so many friends had made the pilgrimage to Boston was a real blessing for me. I realized how much they had been supporting me, even though some still didn't fully understand what I was doing. But just their presence showed their steadfastness and loyalty. Bruce told me that day that a few Penn pals had made a bet that I wouldn't last more than six months. (He refused, however, to tell me who took bets on which side.)

Dan, for his part, made a quick recovery. All he needed was some liquid in him. Everyone, including Dan, had a good laugh about it. He even made it in time for the party. The perfect Jesuit, I joked: misses Mass but makes it for drinks.

The party lasted until dinner, when I went out with my family for a celebratory dinner in Cambridge, along with my soon-to-be brother-in-law and his parents. Then I said my goodbyes. My parents were now less upset than they had been two years prior, since they knew that being a Jesuit wouldn't prevent me from seeing them. The next day I would fly out to Chicago to start the next part of my Jesuit formation—philosophy studies at Loyola University.

After everyone left, I went to the novice director to thank him for the many kindnesses he had shown me over the last two years. Then I started to hand over the cash I had received as gifts from my friends, a standard practice of Jesuit poverty. "You're giving it to the wrong person," Jerry laughed. "You're not a novice any more!"

LATE THAT NIGHT, after we had cleaned up, I went upstairs into the novitiate chapel. It was still warm outside and the ceiling fan stirred a slight breeze in the dark room. I sat down on one of the cushions I prayed on every morning, and was kept company by the candlelight that flickered in front of the small wooden tabernacle.

I never intended to become a Jesuit. My background prepared me to be something completely different from what I had become. When I had started with GE, I thought that I might work there for my entire career. I expected to have lots of money and a healthy bank account, credit cards, a car, and maybe even a mortgage. And I couldn't foresee anything changing my increasingly narrow path.

I didn't think that I would ever work in a hospital and accompany people who were preparing for death. Going to the developing world and working with the sick alongside Mother Teresa's sisters was something other people did. Something I read about or saw in the movies. The homeless were people I would step over and ignore in Manhattan. And I thought I was finished spending time with seventh-graders when I left junior high school. Prayer and real religion was something for holy people, not me. God seemed very far away.

As I sat in the chapel, I was overwhelmed by the blessings and grace I had received over the past years, and the consummate joy that suffused my life as a Jesuit. In just two years, almost despite myself, my life had changed entirely. And completely for the better.

Nothing, as the angel Gabriel said to Mary, is impossible with God.

Acknowledgments

In addition to the people mentioned in this story—my brother novices, friends from school and work, the novitiate staff, friends in Philadelphia, Boston, New York, and Jamaica—there are a few people who were especially helpful in the completion of this book. I am grateful to Jeremy Langford of Sheed & Ward for his initial encouragement and unflagging enthusiasm for this project. As the manuscript neared final completion a number of people were very generous with their advice and comments: Matt Cassidy, S.J., Chris Derby, S.J., John Donohue, S.J., David Donovan, S.J., Avery Dulles, S.J., Steve Katsouros, S.J., Jim Lafontaine, S.J., Bill McNichols, S.J., Vinnie O'Keefe, S.J., John O'Malley, S.J., Ross Pribyl, S.J., Tom Reese, S.J., Bob Reiser, S.J., Brad Schaeffer, S.J., George Williams, S.J., and my sister, Carolyn Martin Buscarino. I am also grateful to Kass Dotterweich of Sheed & Ward for her wise advice, particularly in pointing out areas of the story that deserved further explanation for readers.

Thanks to my Jesuit communities in Nairobi (Loyola House) and New York (America House), where I did the bulk of the writing and editing. Joseph McAuley was also most gracious in helping me type in the final corrections.

Thanks also to my parents, whose support of my Jesuit vocation has grown steadily since my novitiate days and who finally—and happily—vested me in the robes of a priest on ordination day. And I am, of course, enormously grateful to my Jesuit brothers, who make my life one of constant friendship and prayer. The manner may be ordinary, as St. Ignatius wrote, but their companionship has been anything but.

Finally, thanks be to God, who makes all things possible.

James Martin, S.J., is a Jesuit priest, culture editor of *America* magazine, and author of numerous books, including *The Jesuit Guide to (Almost) Everything: A Spirituality for Real Life*, which was a *New York Times* bestseller; *My Life with the Saints*, which won a Christopher Award and was named one of the "Best Books of the Year" by *Publishers Weekly*; *A Jesuit Off-Broadway*; *Becoming Who You Are*; and *This Our Exile*. Before entering the Jesuits in 1988, he graduated from the Wharton School of Business and worked in corporate finance for six years. Father Martin, ordained to the priesthood in 1999, has written for many Catholic magazines, as well as for the *New York Times*, the *Wall Street Journal*, Slate.com and HuffingtonPost.com. He is a frequent commentator in the national and international media on topics of religion and spirituality.